BREATHLESS LOVE

BREATHLESS LOVE

FINDING AND KEEPING YOUR HAPPILY EVER AFTER

REV. DR. TERESA ALLISSA CITRO

DR. NICHOLAS D. YOUNG   DR. LINDA A. KNOWLES

Foreword by
DR. CHARLES E. FARMER

Book and cover design by eBook Prep
www.ebookprep.com
February 2022
ISBN: 978-1-64457-286-3

Rise UP Publications
644 Shrewsbury Commons Ave
Ste 249
Shrewsbury PA 17361
United States of America
www.riseUPpublications.com
Phone: 866-846-5123

FOREWORD

Breathless Love: Finding and Keeping Your Happily Ever After is a biblically-based, solidly rooted application and analysis of true agape love between a man and a woman, husband and wife. The strength of the theme "Beloved" is given from the whole purpose and message of the Scriptures and how the Lord God means for Love to be guided by the Holy Spirit. Definition based is how the book initially begins. I Corinthians 13, better known as the "Love Chapter," is a perfect lead into the outline of the strengths and weaknesses of each man and woman and their love journey together in the book. Here is a listing of these biblical relationships. Abraham and Sarah (Genesis 12) Isaac and Rebekah (Genesis 24) Jacob and Rachel (Genesis 29) King Artaxerxes and Esther (Book of Esther) Boaz and Ruth (Book of Ruth) Shulamite Woman and Song of Solomon King Solomon Love stories, life stories, salvation stories, and redemption stories are the core of this book. One such story is about an elderly couple who some might say were in the sunset of their lives. God led them away from their native homeland to a new land where they were to be fruitful and multiply. It was in their senior years that God told them that the father would be the patriarch of many nations. Their descendants would be like the stars of heaven. This father would be known as a "Friend of God" (James 2:23). The love of a father is also captured in the story of a man who was well advanced in years but still wanted the best wife for his son. He sent his most trusted servant to search for the bride and conduct business on his behalf. One learns a lot about the cultural importance of the birthright, the influence of family traditions, and the many nations God promised. The fulfillment and faithfulness of God's promises and purposes are also exemplified through the love of these couples. Genesis 26, 27, 28. I.

Breathless Love: Finding and Keeping Your Happily Ever After has stories of love, i.e., 14 years of hard labor, deception, stealing, and the true meaning of sex between a man and a woman. God created sex (Genesis 29,30). Through all these situations, the value of a godly wife/spouse is revealed and emphasized. Godly men and women are the glue and molding that holds the key to living a godly life. The next segment of the book focuses on love, intrigue, loyalty, and godly leadership of a young woman, an orphan raised by her cousin/uncle. She is placed in a very unlikely position of authority...for such a time as this (Esther 4:14). She exposes plotters, traitors, and schemers. As a result, she saves a nation, the people of God, from annihilation. Another couple experiences the former life of a wife whose earlier background consisted of godless, demonic, ritualistic practices. Her husband had to demonstrate his real God-like character, faith, and strength. Being in an uncompromising state of action brought this couple a redeemed, restored, and sanctified life (Ruth 1-4). The final epitome of love is captured in the Proverbs 31 woman who has the divine qualities of virtue, wisdom, honor, integrity, beauty, and good business sense. *Breathless Love: Finding and Keeping Your*

Happily Ever After gives us a deeper appreciation of six love stories from the Old Testament of the Holy Bible. Nevertheless, the greatest love story is God the Father's love for mankind through the giving of His Son, the Lord Jesus Christ, Yeshua, our Messiah (John 3:16). Therefore, every love story recorded in this book is a model of the ultimate love of the Father and the Bride of Christ, the Church.

Dr. Charles E. Farmer, Bishop
American Evangelistic Association

INTRODUCTION

This book was birthed during a candid conversation I was having with the Executive Director of Thread of Hope. I was driving down the street as I was talking with her about the seriousness of finding the right life partner.

I began to study these individuals who serve as biblical examples and noted they shared several things in common.

They loved God!

It really starts here. Our love and devotion to God must be the first thing we pursue. The Bible says in Mark 12:30 (KJV), *"And thou shalt love the Lord thy God with all thy heart, and with all thy soul, and with all thy mind, and with all thy strength: this is the first commandment."* When our first love is God, we can be certain He will honor us and will grant us our heart's desires as we are told in Psalm 37:4 (KJV), *"Delight thyself also in the Lord: and he shall give thee the desires of thine heart."*

Everyone has a desire to find their perfect mate and live happily ever after. For that to happen, we must love God. You see, the Bible says in 1 John 4:20 (KJV), *"If a man says, I love God, and hateth his brother, he is a liar: for he that loveth not his brother whom he hath seen, how can he love God whom he hath not seen?"* The people we will discuss in this book were not perfect. They made many mistakes, but because of the love they had for God, they overlooked the imperfections of their partners.

They Chose the Will of God!

One of my favorite Psalms is Psalm 25. Psalm 25:4 (KJV) states, *"Shew me thy ways, O Lord; teach me thy paths."* The couples we will be looking at exhibited this in their lives. They wanted the will of God for their lives. They were willing to be led to their future. In Jeremiah 29:11 (KJV), God says, *"For I know the thoughts that I think toward you, saith the LORD, thoughts of peace, and not of evil, to give you an expected end."* When we study these verses, we clearly see God's desire is to give us an incredible life here on earth.

They Were Faithful in Their Marriage!

The Bible says in Proverbs 20:6-7 (KJV), *"Most men will proclaim everyone his own goodness: but a faithful man who can find? The just man walketh in his integrity: his children are blessed after him."* Do you see the important word here? The faithful man or woman. Who is this type of person? They are devoted to each other. They are loyal no matter what the temptation. They are dedicated, trustworthy, and committed to honoring each other. They are dependable, reliable, and have agreed to make their relationship work for the glory of God. Walking in integrity means running away from the snares Satan has for you. They are what we might call, "true blue." I love that saying. When a man or woman walks in this way, there is a huge promise attached to them. "His (their) children are blessed." Friends, it is this simple obedience and honoring the marriage bed which will bring blessings as seen here in the lives of the people we will talk about.

True love really does exist.

It is a feeling of excitement, mystery, passion, and a devotion to each other. It is adoration and respect towards one another. It is affectionate and charming. It is a deep attachment to each other that is not easily broken. It is a beautiful love affair.

God created us to love deeply. God considers love of its purest kind, the kind that leaves us breathless, so important that He gave us an entire book to understand this mystery between a man and a woman.

The Book of Song of Songs is a true and amazing love story between a man (King Solomon) and a woman (The Shulamite Woman). Love burns, and love desires and fulfills the other. Love is an amazing experience between two people who love each other unconditionally. The Shulamite woman worked in the fields, and her skin was dark compared to the young woman of her days. She was a hard worker, but King Solomon didn't care because he was in love with The Shulamite. The color of her skin didn't matter. It was her heart that he was in love with. His passion for her burned and hers for him. You see, love is important to God. He is the One who created it. Therefore, He wants us to experience it to its fullest.

The world would have us believe it does not exist. Worse, that we can't have it with one person. That is not love. That is called lust, and lust is not fulfilling. Unfortunately, the Church has believed this lie too. Relationships must be maintained. This means you must work at it. It all starts with wanting the will of God more than we want our own. It means we are devoted and give to the one we say we love.

In this book, we will read the most beautiful love stories of all time, real people who experienced amazing love, the love of a lifetime. We can have this kind of love too. We were created to love and be loved. God wants you to experience this kind of love as well. A love that leaves you breathless and wanting for more. Each of the stories of these men and women are extraordinary. They had their ups and downs, they faced challenges so hard, yet the bond of love remained strong between them. Abraham and Sarah, Isaac and Rebekah, Jacob and Rachel, Boaz and Ruth, Queen Esther and King Artaxerxes, and The Shulamite and King Solomon were amazing couples with great destinies and challenges beyond ordinary.

They overcame because of the three things I wrote above. They loved God, chose His will, and were faithful to each other. God honored that and gave them an amazing love story which we still talk about today. We all dream of this kind of love and the truth is, it is yours for the taking. The question is are you willing to go after it with all you got? Are you willing to do it God's way? Are you willing to wait for His leading? According to Ecclesiastes 3:11 (GW), *"He hath made everything beautiful in his time."*

CHAPTER 1

THE FOUNDATION OF LOVE

To understand love, we must clearly understand 1 Corinthians 13. This passage is the basis for what I call real love, the type of love we are all looking for in life.

Who is not looking for the perfect partner in life? All of us want God's best. And to find that person, we must commit ourselves to being the best person God has designed us to be.

The first thing we must understand is we must keep ourselves pure. Do not let the world tell you otherwise. Love waits for the right spouse; it protects this purity to be given after getting married to the one God has for us.

We must give ourselves wholly to purity, meaning we will not allow ourselves to be tempted, and we will not steal this purity from another. I tell my children, "Would you want someone to tempt your future husband/wife? Then your responsibility is to protect yourself from stealing another person's mate and for them to steal what belongs to your future husband or wife."

I am so proud of my two children, Justin and Ellianna. From day one, I spoke to them about waiting for their wedding night to give their purity to their spouse.

At the age of 16, Justin and I went to buy a purity ring. He chose a ruby ring, a woman's ring. He told the jeweler what he was doing, and people heard what Justin said.

He said, "I want a ruby ring because the Bible says, '*Who can find a virtuous woman? For her price is far above rubies,*'" (Proverbs 31:10 KJV).

He wears it around his neck as a reminder that he is wearing her ring on his body, and his love belongs to a young woman who will become his wife. She will receive the ring on their wedding night. I believe as much as Justin is reserving himself for her, God will honor him. God has already chosen his wife, and she will be doing the same.

In a few years, when Ellianna turns 16, she will be picking a ring to present to her husband. In doing that, God will be faithful to her and bring her a man who is pure as well. I am convinced of this because God honors purity. Both my children have told their pediatrician they are not looking for contraceptives because they are going to remain pure until God sends them their spouse. I couldn't be prouder of them because I know God is going to bring them their perfect mates.

This is not just about sex. Love is beyond that. My children understand, once they are married, they are committed to the person they married. This principle applies to all of us. I have heard 1 Corinthians 13 read in most marriage ceremonies we have attended. It serves as the basis for building our love life, truly a love life to be envied. It can be ours for sure.

Song of Songs can and should be ours. God didn't just put it there for us to lust. He put it there for us to enjoy and have. This requires understanding and putting into practice 1 Corinthians 13.

It is called the love chapter for a reason. Love is a powerful emotion, and it is so powerful that it makes us think irrationally at times. However, eventually, the cloud is removed. And if we don't understand the following chapter, we will never succeed in our marriages.

The love God has put together for us can die and be destroyed by our actions.

Let's look carefully at 1 Corinthians Chapter 13.

> I may speak in the languages of humans and of angels. But if I don't have love, I am a loud gong or a clashing cymbal. I may have the gift to speak what God has revealed, and I may understand all mysteries and have all knowledge. I may even have enough faith to move mountains. But if I don't have love, I am nothing. I may even give away all that I have and give up my body to be burned. But if I don't have love, none of these things will help me.
>
> Love is patient. Love is kind. Love isn't jealous. It doesn't sing its own praises. It isn't arrogant. It isn't rude. It doesn't think about itself. It isn't irritable. It doesn't keep track of wrongs. It isn't happy when injustice is done, but it is happy with the truth. Love never stops being patient, never stops believing, never stops hoping, never gives up.
>
> Love never comes to an end. There is the gift of speaking what God has revealed, but it will no longer be used.

There is the gift of speaking in other languages, but it will stop by itself. There is the gift of knowledge, but it will no longer be used. Our knowledge is incomplete and our ability to speak what God has revealed is incomplete. But when what is complete comes, then what is incomplete will no longer be used. When I was a child, I spoke like a child, thought like a child, and reasoned like a child. When I became an adult, I no longer used childish ways. Now we see a blurred image in a mirror. Then we will see very clearly. Now my knowledge is incomplete. Then I will have complete knowledge as God has complete knowledge of me. So these three things remain: faith, hope, and love. But the best one of these is love.

— 1 CORINTHIANS 13

In this chapter, God is clear about what love is. Love does not hurt. Please understand this. I feel very strongly about abuse. I will never agree with anyone who tells me he or she needs to stay in an abusive situation where he or she is being beaten. No way does God want you to honor those vows.

"Love is kind."

This means it is generous, gracious, sympathetic, merciful, considerate, and tender. Look at this list. When your spouse, who in the beginning won your heart, is now having a bad day, can you be merciful and sympathetic? Can you be gracious when your spouse is in a bad mood? Can you be generous in loving your spouse just a little bit more? Being kind when the person doesn't deserve it is all about being kind.

"Love isn't jealous."

This is one of those that most people think doesn't apply to them in their marriage. I say, "Think again." Let us look at the real meaning. It means we cannot be insecure in our relationship. We can't act with suspicion and doubt the love our spouse has for us. We can't allow for mistrust in any way, form, or shape. When we show these things and become so obnoxious that we show that green-eyed envy, it can be a deal-breaker. No relationship can survive this kind of action. God is clearly letting us know that real love is not jealous.

This can apply to being jealous of our spouse's popularity with the opposite sex or in their career. We must cut this destructive behavior immediately. No man or woman can live happily under this behavior. We must turn it around and be mindful, careful, and vigilant to protect the love we have. There are some people who have a personality where people are just attracted to them.

We must be very careful we do not project our fears onto our spouses. God never gave us the spirit of fear. Fear is not of God. However, it should be noted that you do not provoke your spouse to jealousy.

For instance, in today's world, social media has become a huge problem. Husbands and wives do not know how to respect each other on social media. There are certain likes, loves, and comments a married person has no business making. If you are married, do not love or like the photo of a person of the opposite gender and then comment on how beautiful they look, especially when that is the reaction they seek from people. There is a word for this: respect.

"Love does not sing its own praises."

In a marriage, there should never be bragging about how great you are and how horrible the other one is. There is nothing worse than a person who is full of him or herself. No one wants to be around someone who is arrogant and puffed up. Being haughty is nauseating, and a conceited person is the total opposite of love.

Think about the most amazing people you have met. They are humble and meek. I love to be around those kinds of people. They make you feel accepted and heard. They have a way of making you feel absolutely amazing by their actions—what a contrast between the two. I like to look to the positive.

When I look at the word "boastful," I feel anxious just reading about its meaning. Looking at this from a positive perspective brings me joy. Do you understand what I am saying here? Let us look for humility for ourselves no matter what the other person does.

The Bible says in Proverbs 15:2, *"The tongues of wise people give good expression to knowledge."* Then it says in Proverbs 15:4, *"A soothing tongue is a tree of life."* You see, wise people choose their words properly, and their tongue is a tree of life.

We need to breathe life into our marriages, not death. We must constantly encourage our spouses and speak life over them. We do not bring anyone down by boasting about ourselves. It is a destructive thing to do when we tear our spouse down. We are to build up and never tear down.

This especially applies to our husbands. They need to be built up. They need to know we trust them. They are our king, and they are our heroes. It is important to build them up in this way.

In the same way, women need to know they are number one in their husband's lives. A woman needs touch, and she needs to be the queen of her husband's heart. It is especially important for husbands to understand their wives need to be validated, too.

"Love is not rude."

It means we don't get to be disrespectful. Respect in marriage is everything. We do not get to act in an ill-mannered and impolite way.

We don't act uncivilized with each other. This means we do not use insulting and derogatory abusive words to each other. We are not to act without manners and be disrespectful to the one we say we love.

The word "rude" means abusive; it is a terrible way to treat another human. We never have the right to act this way. God is watching, and He takes good notes of our actions, especially towards our spouses.

God holds marriages at a remarkably high calling. We are responsible for how we treat each other in our marriages. Let us not be insulting to each other. Let us instead praise the other and always act with excellent manners towards each other.

"Love does not think about itself."

In other words, it is not selfish. It is not self-centered, all about them and only their needs. It is not self-serving (what's in it for me) or self-seeking. This is a very uncaring attitude, and no one wants to be married to a thoughtless person.

In looking at the word "more," the word "greedy" came up. A selfish person is a greedy person. It is all about looking out for number one, in other words, themselves. God is saying here that love is unselfish. What a spouse should ask is, "what selfless acts can I do to show my love to my spouse? How can I serve him or her? How can I be considerate and charitable towards the one I love?"

"Love is not irritable."

People can become irritable so quickly. God is warning us against this. It is all about our mood. We can become grumpy over the most ridiculous things. Being annoyed easily is a bad trait. In a marriage, we can't allow ourselves to put down the ones we love by our moody and grouchy attitudes. We are better than this.

The Bible says, *"A short-tempered person acts stupidly, and a person who plots evil is hated."* I think this is self-explanatory. We tell our children never to call anyone stupid. The Bible clearly states a short-tempered person (an irritable one) is stupid. We have no room in our marriages to be stupid. Pardon my word here, please.

"Love does not keep track of wrongs."

We must forget and forgive what was done in the past, and it cannot ever come back to be thrown into the face of our spouse. When we forgive, we forgive the offense, and we never bring it up again. It is sinful to do this because the Bible says in Micah 7:19, *"You will be merciful to us once again. You will trample our sins under-foot and send them to the bottom of the sea!"* If God can show us mercy and send our sins to the bottom of the sea, how dare we keep hold of the sins that were done unto us!

Do you know there are over 25 Bible verses regarding forgiveness? The word 'forgive' appears 42 times in the Old Testament and 33 Times in the New Testament, and from the NIV, 75 times. God tells us to forgive 70 X 7, meaning we do not keep track of how many times we forgive; we always forgive..

The best marriages are those who can forgive an offense. People often take offense when another person says something, and it is interpreted as offensive; however, the person never meant it as such.

The Bible clearly says, *"Love does not keep track of wrongs."* This means we forgive. And we forgive the way God told us to, by letting it go and never dragging it back up. Have you ever seen a river or lake dragged up? I have, and it stinks very badly. Leave the offense in the bottom of the sea.

"Love isn't happy when injustice is done, but it is happy with the truth."

Love thrives in justice and in truth. In other words, it abhors corruption, exploitation, prejudice, cruelty, unfairness, and intolerance toward each other. It hates all wrongdoings. It loves sincerity, honesty, truthfulness, being authentic with each other, and being forthright with each other in a respectable manner. These are real-life successful marriages right here, using these attributes to build your marriage. Be honest and truthful with each other.

Being real is so important to the growth of a marriage. Hiding things never works; they come back to kill and destroy.

"Love never stops being patient."

Do you see what I see? Love started with being patient, and it ends with being patient. This is a double wow moment for me, and it should be for you too. God started this love chapter with patience, and He ends with it. You see, love is all about being patient with each other.

We all have issues to work on. We need to love each other in the imperfections because it is the love of God and the love of our spouses that should spur us on to reach for the prize of having the perfect marriage. The perfect marriage is made up of imperfect and flawed people. Therefore, we must work hard to be patient with the one we love and the one we choose to live with for the rest of our lives.

God couldn't explain it better by starting with patience and ending with patience. Take a look at the end of this *"Love never stops being patient never stops believing, never stops hoping, never gives up."* You see it? It *never stops believing* in the one we love, it *never stops hoping* for the best in the one we love, and, my all-time favorite, *never gives up*. Love never ever gives up.

Now, do you understand why I believe no one can have a successful marriage without fully understanding 1 Corinthians 13?

God gave us a road map of what to do and not to do when it comes to love. The real question is will you abide by it? It doesn't matter what the other person does; it matters what you do.

God honors faithfulness. God will take care of the one who practices what He says for that person to do. If we do what He is asking us to do in His Word, then God, in His loving mercy, will honor our actions. Either He will heal the marriage, or He will open the door for us to go. Regardless of how He chooses to do it, our calling is to obey His Word and put into practice what He commands us to do.

The Word of God is powerful, and it will prove to be faithful in our lives when we obey and do what it is in it.

In the coming chapters, we will look at the love stories of couples in the Bible that exemplify this love chapter. I don't know about you, but I want to be loved as a woman the same way these men loved their wives. And, if you are a man reading this, then you should want a beautiful wife who honors and loves her husband as the women in these stories honor and love their husbands.

Let us go after the Word of God and apply it in our lives so that we can experience true love between us and our spouses, implementing the true meaning of what love is into our marriages and depositing, daily, and as often as we get the chance, all these beautiful things about what love is and rejecting and getting rid of what love isn't. Love is powerful and love is beautiful; and Song of Songs is very real.

Set yourself as a seal upon the heart of the one you love, and never allow anything or anyone to steal it.

Discussion For Couples and Groups:

1. As you see it, what are your strengths and weaknesses?
2. Now ask the Holy Spirit, "What are my strengths and weaknesses?"
3. What are your companion's strengths and weaknesses? (Please understand this question is not meant to tear down or hurt your companion. Each is responsible for his or her own actions.)
4. If you are married, is there a character trait which concerns you that you didn't see before you were married? If you are not married, is there a character trait your companion has that concerns you?
5. Is there something you can do to help your companion build up the weaknesses that concern you so that the weaknesses become strengthened? (For instance, if you know your companion is notoriously late for everything, what can you do to help them be on time?)

6. How can the two of you work together to help each other
   with the other's weaknesses?
7. In any relationship, appreciation is essential. What do
   you love the most about your companion, and do you
   honestly show your companion you appreciate him
   or her?

CHAPTER 2

ABRAHAM AND SARAH

Abraham and Sarah were a couple with deep love, respect, and honor for each other. A love story we surely can admire. They made huge mistakes, but their love was deep, real, and alive. They practiced 1 Corinthians 13 without the chapter being written at that time. We can learn much from their relationship.

Let's pick up the story shown in Genesis from the time they packed up and left Ur.

> So Abram left, as the Lord had told him, and Lot went with him. Abram was 75 years old when he left Haran.
> Abram set out for Canaan. He took along his wife Sarai, his nephew Lot, and all the possessions they had accumulated and the servants they had acquired in Haran.
>
> — GENESIS 12: 4-5

Imagine being 65 years old and your husband tells you, "Hey, Sweetheart, God spoke to me and told me to leave this place. I don't know where we are going. He said He will show us along the way. But don't worry, He is going to make us into a huge nation." I don't know about you, but I would freak out.

Sarah had every right to protest and question his sanity, but she didn't. She trusted her husband. I want you to get this... Marriage is all about trust. Trust in the person you married who is the priest and head of your household.

Let's be real here. Traveling then was not like today, traveling by car, bus, train, or airplane. It was traveling by camel with no such thing as hotels and restaurants along the way. This journey was straight in the middle of a desert. No hospitals, no police stations, no hair salons, never mind nail salons.

There is no evidence of her protesting. She followed the man she loved. She could have said, "Well, Babe, I have to go pray and ask God to confirm to me, too. I am your wife, after all, you know. I need to make this decision along with you, too."

No! She packed and followed her husband. We can learn a lot from her. The truth of the matter is she was his wife and recognized he was the head of their household.

Sarah trusted the man she was married to for a very long time to lead her to the Promised Land. Most women want to be led by the man they love. Abraham wasn't always leading into great and exciting things. Sarah didn't protest because she was made to feel secure by Abraham and the love and respect he had for her.

The first time we see Abraham making a really bad move and letting Sarah down is in Genesis 12...

> There was a famine in the land. Abram went to Egypt to
> stay awhile because the famine was severe. When he
> was about to enter Egypt, Abram said to his wife Sarai,
> 'I know that you're a beautiful woman. When the Egyp-
> tians see you, they'll say, 'This is his wife!' Then they'll
> kill me but let you live. Please say that you're my sister.
> Then everything will be alright for me, and because of
> you I will live.' When Abram arrived in Egypt, the
> Egyptians saw how very beautiful his wife was. When
> Pharaoh's officials saw her, they raved about her to
> Pharaoh, so Sarai was taken to Pharaoh's palace. Every-
> thing went well for Abram because of her, and he was
> given sheep, cattle, donkeys, male and female slaves,
> and camels.
>
> — GENESIS 12:10-16

Imagine being Sarah. She left her home and most of her possessions because she couldn't take everything with her, as they would
be traveling by foot and with their camel. She left many things she
loved. It is not so hard to imagine this.

In addition, she left her family, friends, and community. She gave
everything to her husband and trusted him with her very life.
They were a team, a team with a great promise.

Then, after all that, you are told by your husband, "Tell the Egyp-
tians you are my sister so they will not kill me." Am I alone in
believing how devastating this would have been for her? Are you
like me asking yourself, "What would I have done?"

Imagine the fear she had to endure as Pharaoh took her in as his
wife. Abraham was paid handsomely for her. He acquired lots of

possessions because of her. Sarah was a beautiful woman, and Pharaoh desired her.

I am sure Sarah cried many tears. She was abandoned and treated cruelly by her husband. The man that was supposed to protect, honor, and take care of her, just allowed her to be taken by an Egyptian Pharaoh.

Imagine when she was taken into the palace and began preparing before being taken by Pharaoh into his bedroom. The feelings she must have gone through are too hard for any of us to even begin to say, "We understand."

God, however, moved in and protected her. He was watching over her; He was making sure she would not be defiled in any way, form, or shape.

Now, I am not saying Abraham purposely tried to hurt her or that he didn't love her because we know this is not the case. He loved Sarah.

Abraham's problem was fear. He was afraid of being killed, so he made Sarah tell a half-truth. It was true she was his half-sister, but she was his wife. He failed her.

She never said anything about this to Abraham, nor did she act in any way disrespectful towards him once Pharaoh realized she was Abraham's wife. When Pharaoh found out, he was angry, and he let her go and let them leave the area. God was definitely with Sarah, but Abraham paid a huge price for those possessions Pharaoh gave them.

May I suggest that our sins cost us something greater down the line? Abraham's decision to go to Egypt had consequences. In a word, Hagar. He inherited Hagar. Did God tell him to take Hagar? There is nowhere in Scripture that says for Abraham to take Hagar with him. Hagar became a stumbling block to him and his wife. Sarah decided to use Hagar to produce Abraham's heir, and it backfired. We are still paying for the consequences of that sin to this day.

As if the first time wasn't bad enough, in Genesis 20, Abraham once more does the same thing...

> Abraham moved to the Negev and settled between Kadesh
> and Shur. While he was living in Gerar, Abraham told
> everyone that his wife Sarah was his sister. So King
> Abimelech of Gerar sent men to take Sarah.
>
> — GENESIS 20:1-2

I don't know about anyone else, but this would have sent me over the edge. Let's face it, what woman would not have to deal with trust issues now? Any other woman would have probably said, "Really, Abraham? You didn't learn the first time from your lie and deceit?" Here she is hearing her husband telling everyone she was his sister and never admitting this beautiful woman God had given him was the love of his life.

Imagine having to relive the nightmare, "Surely, this can't be happening to me again?" Once again, God protected her. He never allowed King Abimelech to touch her. She was never defiled by him. Again, there is no mention of Sarah ever saying one word against her husband.

Sarah practiced the verses in 1 Corinthians 13...

> Love is patient. Love is kind. Love isn't jealous. It doesn't
> sing its own praises. It isn't arrogant. It isn't rude. It
> doesn't think about itself. It isn't irritable. It doesn't
> keep track of wrongs. It isn't happy when injustice is
> done, but it is happy with the truth. Love never stops
> being patient, never stops believing, never stops
> hoping, and never gives up. Love never comes to
> an end.
>
> — 1 CORINTHIANS 13:4-8

Who would disagree that Sarah wasn't patient and kind towards her husband? She didn't think about herself and the hurt she would have to endure by being taken by two very powerful men, both a pharaoh and a king.

She didn't become irritable and didn't keep track of the wrongs done unto her. She rejoiced when God delivered her and moved forward. She never stopped being patient with her husband. She never stopped believing in her husband, never stopped hoping for the best in him, and never gave up on this wonderful man God called, "A righteous man, and a friend." Never did this beautiful love story ever come to an end.

The day came when Abraham respected her wishes—the day she asked him to send away Hagar and her son. God himself told Abraham, "Listen to your wife, Sarah."

There was another listening and taking note of her actions. It was God! God honored Sarah. He wasn't going to let Hagar continue to mock her and cause trouble between the two sons.

However, before that, God performed one of the most incredible miracles. He gave her a son at the age of 90 and protected her, and honored her.

God knew the character of Sarah when He changed her name from Sarai to Sarah, meaning "Princess." She was a princess not just in beauty but in actions, loving, respecting, honoring, and supporting a man who made some terrible choices.

Abraham knew the kind of woman he was married to, and he knew he needed her protection. I am sure he wasn't happy to ask her to pretend she was only his sister. I am sure he was praying up a storm as much as she was for God to deliver her from being defiled by those two men.

Abraham was a man that was being broken and then reshaped into the man God was calling him to be. He had some issues he had to deal with God about, as well as trusting God. He wasn't always led by God. God never told him to go to Egypt. He panicked because of the famine and went down to Egypt. There were things God was working on and working out in Abraham's life and character.

Sarah wasn't all that innocent either. She knew God made the promise of a child, but she didn't trust her husband's leading. She made him go into her handmaiden and sleep with her to bring forth a child. What a terrible mistake, and the world still is suffering from it.

That mistake cost her a lot of pain. Hagar became very mean and arrogant towards Sarah once she became pregnant.

The day came when Abraham had to learn a very important lesson. He had to take his son, Isaac, whom he loved, his only son, and sacrifice him. This is where we find Abraham finally willing to trust God. God miraculously provided a ram for him to sacrifice instead of his son.

Finally, something else took place when he left to sacrifice Isaac. He never told Sarah what he was going to do. Finally, he protected his wife.

Abraham and Sarah made mistakes, but the love they had is something we still talk about more than 2,000 years later. Isn't this the type of love we are all looking for?

You can have all the attributes spoken of in the Love Chapter of 1 Corinthians and still have to work on them because they may also be weaknesses. The passage says, *"Love is patient,"* and while patience may be your strength, it can also be your weakness and therefore need to be worked on. For instance: You may be patient with co-workers, but you may be impatient with your spouse.

Let's look at the strengths and weaknesses of Abraham and Sarah, how they complemented each other, and how they used those strengths in some areas but not in all areas. When they didn't implement their strengths fully, that's when they made major mistakes.

Sarah's Message for Women

Patient Sarah, who had followed her husband, leaving everything behind to travel to an unknown land, was passed off to two kings as his sister. Still, suddenly she becomes impatient, waiting for God to give her the promised child. Impatient Sarah then hands her servant Hagar to Abraham to have relations with him to have a child: Biggest mistake with consequences to follow.

Sarah's Strengths	Sarah's Weaknesses
Obedient (1 Peter 3:6)	Impatient (Genesis 16:1-5)
Respect (Genesis 18:12)	Jealous of Hagar (Genesis 16:4)
Patient (Genesis 12:4)	
Didn't think about herself	
(Genesis 13:1)	
Isn't happy when injustice is done	
(Genesis 21:8-10)	

The world has not understood the word "Obedience" when it comes to marriage. When we promise to love and obey our husbands, we are saying, "I'm going to respect him. I'm going to willingly support him and all that God has called him to do because his blessing will be paid back and fall upon our children and me.

I will know my place to be meek and quiet in my criticisms. I will refrain from bringing him down but rather use all truthful words to build him up. I will remind him that he excels in whatever God has called him to do.

I will stand in agreement with his decisions like Sarah did, even in his foolish decisions like when he gave her to two other men (Making this statement doesn't mean you go against God's laws and commandments, nor do we break the laws of the land. Today, God gave us a Bible for us to follow. I'm not saying go out and commit sin. I am saying to do what God tells you to do in His Word, no more, no less).

For example: Your husband, at the age of 45, decides he no longer wants to be in his field of work, and you might be freaking out at his desire but support and encourage him.

Be quiet about trying to stop his will and take your battle on your knees in prayer and pray that God will lead your husband to make godly decisions. God will hear your prayer. He hears the prayer of the righteous, and He answers.

Every man desires the respect and honor of his wife as she trusts him to make decisions, believing he can do anything and everything to lead her and the family.

Ladies, the word "obedience" means all these things, plus we are to revere, yield to, and respect our husband. The biggest mistake women make is not understanding that it is all about respect and honor, yielding to his God-given authority.

A friend of mine once told me during a difficult time in her marriage that she was standing at the kitchen sink washing dishes when it seemed like Heaven opened up. Then it dawned on her, "Lily, you idiot, God gave man the leadership of the home, giving him all the responsibility for leadership, and God holds him accountable for his leadership.

God did women a favor. You are responsible for your own actions and words toward your husband. Your husband is responsible for all the rest. Give him the control he needs that you are trying to take away.

As a very strong-willed woman, I fully embrace and understand this principle because for a successful wife, you, as a woman, better possess and understand this. The Word of God is very clear that a wise woman builds her home while a foolish woman tears it down with her own hands.

My prayer, as a woman, is that you, my Fellow Sisters, walk in all authority and fully understand the Word of God: Because your blessing, and that of your children, critically depends on your obedience (reverence, yield, respect) to God and to your husband.

Abraham's Message for Men

Abraham's Strengths	Abraham's Weaknesses
Obedient (Genesis 26:5)	Thought about himself (Genesis 12:10-20; 20:1-18)
Patient (Hebrews 6:15)	Irritable (Genesis 16:6)
Never gave up hope in God's Promises (Genesis 12:1-2)	
Not Jealous (Genesis 12:10-20; 20:1-18)	

Just as the world does not understand the word "obedience," people don't understand the word "love".

The language that women respond very well to is appreciation. She wants to feel that you are devoted to her because she has given her life to honor, respect, and yield to you. She wants you to protect her dignity and honor, and she wants you to hold her in high esteem.

Recognize her accomplishments because what she does is to do her best to bring you honor.

She wants you to cherish her as a precious jewel. She wants to know she is the only one, which means she wants your loyalty. Your faithfulness to her is of great importance.

She wants you to be passionate towards her. Believe it or not, she wants the passion. Understand, like you have your needs, so does she. That means you both lay down your desires one for another.

In this story, Abraham, by compromising Sarah to save his own life, failed to protect her honor and her dignity. Thank God that He saw Sarah's love, respect, and reverence toward her husband—God protected her.

Thank God those men never violated her. I believe Abraham recognized the great sacrifice made. I also believe it was because of her love that she never said one word to him regarding him giving her away to two men. Her silence on this issue spoke loudly.

Men, may I suggest to you that if you want to be king of every domain in your marriage, you better treat her as queen of your everything.

Contrary to popular belief, the majority of women, especially godly women, are not after your money or your fancy cars. They are looking for your fervent love, and they are looking for your leadership.

They want to feel secure with you as the head of the household, leading your home in a godly manner that brings about blessings and the success God has for you as a couple and as a family.

In the following chapters, keep in mind what women want and what men want.

It is all about submission. Submission is a beautiful word that has gotten a bad reputation. But I am here to tell you that the word "Submission" is wrapped up in everything men and women want.

> Place yourselves under each other's authority out of
> respect for Christ,...

> — EPHESIANS 5:21

Through all these challenges in a relationship, we learn how to achieve the greatest of all love.

CHAPTER 3
ISAAC AND REBEKAH

The love story of Isaac and Rebekah is my favorite love story in the Bible.

Abraham had become an old man. Sarah, his wife, passed away. Isaac was now 40 years old and still not married. Abraham wanted his son to marry a godly and good woman. He asked his servant, whom he trusted with everything he owned, to go and find a wife for his beloved son, Isaac.

We see a father trusting his servant to find a wife for his son, a young woman seeking the will of God, and a young man trusting God to bring him his life partner.

Let's look together at this incredible love story and the most beautiful marriage in the history of the Bible.

> So Abraham said to the senior servant of his household
> who was in charge of all that he owned, 'Take a solemn
> oath. I want you to swear by the Lord God of heaven
> and earth that you will not get my son a wife from the

daughters of the Canaanites among whom I'm living.
Instead, you will go to the land of my relatives and get a
wife for my son Isaac.'

— GENESIS 24:2-4

What a commission! He was sending him back to his original
place of birth to pick a bride from the land of his relatives. In His
ultimate love matchmaking, God led him on an incredible journey
to Isaac's future wife, Rebekah.

For Isaac to have a blessed marriage, Abraham knew Isaac had to
marry a woman who feared God. If you want a successful
marriage, you must pick a partner who loves and honors God.

Marriage is hard work, and it comes with many challenges. If the
people within the marriage do not submit themselves to God first,
they will never submit to each other.

God had taken Abraham out of the land of Ur and promised to
make him into a vast nation. From Abraham, God would make a
nation that was holy unto Him. It was important for Isaac to marry
a woman who honored and loved God with her life.

The Bible talks about wives leading their husbands away from
serving Him. Isaac had a special calling on his life. He was the
child promised to Abraham and Sarah by God. And he would
continue in the lineage of birthing God's special people, the Jewish
nation.

The promise of God coming to pass required the right wife for
Isaac. This is not just for them; it's for us too. God wants to build a
holy family from us. A family who will honor God and love each
other to be used for His glory and honor.

The servant asked him, 'What if the woman doesn't want to come back to this land with me? Should I take your son all the way back to the land you came from?' 'Make sure that you do not take my son back there,' Abraham said to him. 'The Lord God of heaven took me from my father's home and the land of my family. He spoke to me and swore this oath: 'I will give this land to your descendants.' 'God will send his angel ahead of you, and you will get my son a wife from there. If the woman doesn't want to come back with you, then you'll be free from this oath that you swear to me. But don't take my son back there.' So the servant did as his master Abraham commanded and swore the oath to him concerning this. Then the servant took ten of his master's camels and left, taking with him all of his master's best things. He traveled to Aram Naharaim, Nahor's city."

— GENESIS 24:5-10

Can you understand why the servant would be nervous?

"What if the woman doesn't want to come back with me? Should I take your son with me?"

One would think that Abraham would have agreed to have his son go. Instead, he says, *"Do not take my son Isaac with you."*

We don't know for sure why Abraham was adamant not to take Isaac. It could be because he was very wealthy, and something could happen to him. It could be that Abraham was old and maybe didn't want to be left alone, or it could be that he didn't want His son Isaac to be tempted by settling there in Ur.

I don't know for sure, but I find it interesting that the next thing he says is, *"The Lord God of heaven took me from my father's home and the land of my family. He spoke to me and swore this oath: 'I will give this land to your descendants.'"*

This could have been the issue. The wrong woman and her family could have convinced him to stay in the land of his father. That was not what God had instructed and led Abraham to do.

Then Abraham makes an incredible statement, *"God will send his angel ahead of you, and you will get my son a wife from there."* Abraham was God's friend. God had proven over and over to Abraham that He would bless him and make his descendants great. God walked with Abraham. Abraham had no doubt God had already picked a wife for Isaac.

How can I be sure? First of all, Isaac was now approximately the age of 40. This was late for a man to be married. Usually, around 30 years of age, they were already married.

We learn here that we don't have to be in a hurry. We trust God for His perfect time.

> He makes everything beautiful in His time." We can learn
> from this. Better we take our time than be married to
> the wrong person.
>
> — ECCLESIASTES 3:11

His servant packed ten camels with the most expensive gifts and left to find a wife for Isaac.

Notice something important here. There is no mention at all about what Isaac had to say. There was no meeting between Abraham, Isaac, and the servant. Isaac is missing in action. Where was Isaac? Was it that Isaac didn't care at all? He never attended that meeting, nor is there any mention of Abraham telling the servant what kind of woman Isaac was looking for.

You don't find Isaac objecting to this. He, of course, had to see ten camels packed with the most valuable things owned by his family. We don't read anywhere about him giving any kind of comments about this, such as, "Hey, make sure you find me a woman that has blue eyes or blond hair. Make sure she is skinny, or make sure she is tall. Be sure her face looks like this, and her body looks like that." Nothing. Absolutely nothing.

This is why this story is my favorite. Being loved for you and not for what you look like is every woman's dream. Being cherished and loved deep within a man's heart is what we look for.

I am not a man, but I venture to say a man wants to be loved for him, not for what kind of provision he can make for his wife or if he is tall enough or has rippling muscles bulging from his shirt.

Don't get me wrong. There must be an attraction. But our world is more into what a person looks like than the character of the person.

We ladies should want an Isaac. He trusted God to bring his wife. Remember, he watched God provide for his father, and he was the one who was put on the altar when the greatest test of faith took place between Abraham and God.

Isaac knew beyond a shadow of a doubt that God was going to bring him the love of his life, and he had waited for her a long time—ten extra years to get her. During that time, if you married past the age of thirty, you were considered old.

The Bible describes him as a quiet and peaceful man, great attributes to hold as a man. He wasn't a hot-tempered man. He was a man who loved peace.

The servant finally arrived at Abraham's hometown.

> The servant had the camels kneel down outside the city by the well. It was evening, when the women would go out to draw water. Then he prayed, 'Lord, God of my master Abraham, make me successful today. Show your kindness to Abraham. Here I am standing by the spring, and the girls of the city are coming out to draw water. I will ask a girl, 'May I please have a drink from your jar?' If she answers, 'Have a drink, and I'll also water your camels,' let her be the one you have chosen for your servant Isaac. This way I'll know that you've shown your kindness to my master.' Before he had finished praying, Rebekah came with her jar on her shoulder. She was the daughter of Bethuel, son of Milcah, who was the wife of Abraham's brother Nahor. The girl was a very attractive virgin. No man had ever had sexual intercourse with her. She went down to the spring, filled her jar, and came back. The servant ran to meet her and said, 'Please give me a drink of water.' 'Drink, sir,' she said. She quickly lowered her jar to her hand and gave him a drink. When she had finished giving him a drink, she said, "I'll also keep drawing water for your camels until they've had enough to drink.' So she quickly emptied her jar into the water trough, ran back to the well to draw more water, and drew enough for all his camels. The man was silently

watching her to see whether or not the Lord had made his trip successful.

— GENESIS 24:11-21

Ladies, observe this. *"The man was silently watching her to see whether or not the Lord had made his trip successful."*

Please understand before we go any further: You do not know who is watching you. Real men want a person of character and integrity as much as a real woman wants the same.

Our character is all we have, and we must protect it against all odds. Do not allow your character to be stolen from you. A respectable man or woman will not allow the other to lose integrity and honor. Be careful who you trust. The angel of the Lord is encamped around His people. He will not allow you to stumble. Be alert, women, and act like ladies.

And men, stay your course and act like gentlemen.

God set it all up. Then here comes Rebekah to fill her jar of water. I love Rebekah. She is Miss Confident.

We see what she does, *"When she had finished giving him a drink, she said, "I'll also keep drawing water for your camels until they've had enough to drink."*

Rebekah is an inspiration to me! The Bible says she was very beautiful.

However, Abraham's servant was looking beyond physical beauty. He wanted Isaac to have a woman who had inner beauty.

He asked God to show him kindness and help him find a wife for Isaac. God loves it when we ask for His perfect will.

The Word of God says that *before* he had finished praying, Rebekah came out with her jar. He asked her for water, which was very customary to provide water for those who asked.

But she went beyond that. She took the initiative to also give a drink to ten camels.

Do you know how much a camel drinks? Anywhere between 30-50 gallons. She had ten thirsty camels. That is close to 500 gallons of water she had to draw from the well. Does this tell you what kind of strength this woman had? She had to let her bucket down and then pull the water up. I can't even imagine that.

Rebekah inspires me, and she should inspire you too. You see, this young woman had character. She had outward beauty and inner beauty.

In fact, her behavior reveals many beautiful attributes. She exhibited much kindness. She was thoughtful, generous, caring, kindhearted, considerate, compassionate, and humane toward the camels. You see, she saw a need, then she took charge and met the need.

To be the wife of a prominent, wealthy man whom God has chosen to bring forth a great people, you must be strong in character.

She had it all—beauty, kindness, love, compassion, and self-respect. She took the initiative. She didn't have to be asked. She saw what needed doing, and she did it. Eliezer, Abraham's servant, saw that this woman had a heart for doing far more than the bare minimum. He saw the servant spirit in her, and this won his admiration.

After the camels had finished drinking, she got the biggest surprise of her life.

> When the camels had finished drinking, the man took out
> a gold nose ring weighing a fifth of an ounce and two
> gold bracelets weighing four ounces. He asked, 'Whose
> daughter are you? Please tell me whether there is room
> in your father's house for us to spend the night.' She
> answered him, 'I'm the daughter of Bethuel, son of
> Milcah and Nahor. We have plenty of straw and feed
> for your camels and room for you to spend the night.'
> The man knelt, bowing to the Lord with his face
> touching the ground. He said, 'Praise the Lord, the God
> of my master Abraham. The Lord hasn't failed to be
> kind and faithful to my master. The Lord has led me on
> this trip to the home of my master's relatives.' The girl
> ran and told her mother's household about these
> things. Rebekah had a brother whose name was Laban.
> He saw the nose ring and the bracelets on his sister's
> wrists and heard her tell what the man had said to her.
> Immediately, Laban ran out to the man by the spring.
> He came to the man, who was standing with the camels
> by the spring. He said, 'Come in, you whom the Lord
> has blessed. Why are you standing out here? I have
> straightened up the house and made a place for the
> camels.'
>
> — GENESIS 24:22-31

When we are busy doing what God puts in front of us, He takes care of the rest. Rebekah's action changed her life forever. She became the wife of Isaac and played a huge role in being the mother and grandmother of the Twelve Tribes of Israel.

Eliezer spoke with her father and brother as the story continues, and they agreed to the marriage proposal. However, it doesn't end here. Here is the next scene.

> Then he and the men who were with him ate and drank and spent the night. When they got up in the morning, he said, 'Let me go back to my master.'" Her brother and mother replied, 'Let the girl stay with us ten days or so. After that she may go.' He said to them, 'Don't delay me now that the Lord has made my trip success-ful. Let me go back to my master.' So, they said, 'We'll call the girl and ask her.' They called for Rebekah and asked her, 'Will you go with this man?' She said, 'Yes, I'll go.'
>
> — GENESIS 24:54-58

Rebekah didn't play games. When the proposal was made and the marriage arranged, she could have milked it, but she didn't. She was serious. When her family asked her, and we are talking about the next morning, she said, 'Yes, I'll go.' Her mind was made up.

Like Isaac, she never asked, "Wait, please, what does Isaac look like? Does he have dreamy big brown eyes? Does he have dimples? Is he tall, dark, and handsome?" Nothing! She takes the same approach as Isaac. That is so amazing to me. Like Isaac, she was trusting God to pick the right mate. God certainly honored that.

Rebekah left with Eliezer, making the journey to her man and to her new home.

Here's the account of the day they met.

> Isaac had just come back from Beer Lahai Roi, since he was
> living in the Negev. Toward evening Isaac went out into
> the field to meditate. When he looked up, he saw
> camels coming. When Rebekah saw Isaac, she got
> down from her camel. She asked the servant, 'Who is
> that man over there coming through the field to meet
> us?' 'That is my master,' the servant answered. Then
> she took her veil and covered herself. The servant
> reported to Isaac everything he had done. Isaac took
> her into his mother Sarah's tent. He married Rebekah.
> She became his wife, and he loved her. So Isaac was
> comforted after his mother's death.
>
> — GENESIS 24:62-67

Picture this scene. Isaac just got back home, and he went out to the field to meditate. This means to pray. He was out there praying. I am sure he asked God to protect his wife wherever she was and bring her to him safe and sound. He would be praying for a successful trip for his servant and his future wife. He was praying for her and her safety, and he didn't even know her.

We can learn a lot from this story. Are we praying for our future mate? Are we praying for God's protection over them? Do we love enough to pray that God watches, protects, and blesses the one we will marry someday?

This is important. God will honor us when we love our future spouses before they even enter our eyesight.

Meanwhile, the entourage was arriving. Isaac saw the camels arriving. The anticipation must have been unbelievable. Then, the camels came closer, and Rebekah saw a man coming towards them to meet them.

She caught his eye. She wanted to know who he was. Could it be that she fell in love with the man who was walking towards her?

God would never bring someone to anyone that the person wouldn't find attractive and fall in love with. This story is too amazing to think anything different.

She quickly respected her man after Eliezer told her that Isaac was his master. You see, ladies, we must respect our man. This represents not just the custom of that day. It represents honoring and respecting the man God has given you. Do you want to be loved and treated like gold? Respect your husband. Respect the man you are engaged to. It is all about respect and honor.

Isaac took Rebekah, and he married her. He took her to his mother's tent, and the Bible says, *"He loved her!"*

Wow! I love this story.

Did they live happily ever after? No. They did not.

She gives birth to twins, and we learn that God tells her, not Isaac, that the second to come out will serve the first. They would be rivals. This is exactly what took place. She convinces her son, Jacob, to take the blessing from Esau.

I often wonder what happened. I believe Isaac was going to just bless Esau because he was the firstborn of the twins, which was tradition.

God had said, *"Jacob would serve Esau."* In this deception, Rebekah protected her husband's legacy. Isaac, for whatever reason, was going to bless the child that didn't care about his birthright. God cared, and God made sure the right child received the blessing.

I wish they could have talked about it and come up with the right thing to do, to follow the will of God. That didn't happen. But Isaac never yelled at Rebekah or said anything mean to her.

This couple, just like Abraham and Sarah, wasn't perfect. But the love, admiration, and respect were deep and meaningful, and God blessed them. We can learn much from this love story.

Rebekah's Lessons for Women

Rebekah's Strengths	Rebekah's Weaknesses
Kind (Genesis 24:18-20)	Deceitful (Genesis 26:6-11, 27:5-17)
Patient (Genesis 25:19-24)	Happy When Injustice Was Done (Genesis 27:1-30)
Didn't think about herself (Genesis 24:61-67)	
Not happy when injustice was done (Genesis 27:1-10)	
Never gave up on her family (Genesis 27:46-28:1-5)	

Isaac's Lessons for Men

Isaac's Strengths	Isaac's Weaknesses
Kind (Genesis 24:62-67)	Arrogance (Genesis 27:1-4)
Patient (Genesis 25:20)	Impatient (Genesis 27:1-4)
Wasn't Rude (Genesis 27:46)	
Didn't keep track of wrongs (Genesis 28:1-4)	
Wasn't jealous (Genesis 26:6-11)	

The world does not understand that cultures and traditions stop at the Cross. Being the founder and president of a ministry and being the CEO of a nonprofit education organization has taught me many lessons about culture and tradition.

Although cultures are rich in traditions, it doesn't mean they are biblically correct. In fact, I have found traditions and cultures are often contrary to the Word of God in many, if not all, nations.

To understand what caused Rebekah's deceitfulness, you need to understand the culture of the time. The word "blessing" is so important that it is mentioned over 600 times in the Old Testament. There are other terms related to the word "blessing" which means "to kneel" because one would be kneeling down to receive a blessing.

> Instead, he must recognize the son of the wife he doesn't love as the firstborn. He must give that son a double portion of whatever he owns. That son is the very first son he had. The rights of the firstborn son are his.

> — DEUTERONOMY 21:17

This is an incredible teaching about the firstborn. Abraham received the covenant promise. God promised him that he would become the father of many nations and establish the blessing for the people of God, the Nation of Israel.

Although Abraham's first son was Ishmael, the blessing belonged to Isaac as it is in the story here. Esau did not receive the blessing. But his twin brother, Jacob, did receive the blessing. Jacob's first son, Reuben, did not receive the blessing, but rather Joseph, Rachel's son, received the blessing instead.

Joseph's first son, Manasseh, did not receive the blessing, but instead, Ephraim, his brother, did.

When it comes to the tribes that were numbered, Reuben's tribe was not mentioned, but Levi's tribe (considered the firstborn of Israel) was the first mentioned.

I want you to catch something very important in all of this. God does not fall in line with culture or traditions. In all of these blessings, nothing was followed according to culture or tradition.

Abraham and Isaac tried to hand the blessing down to their children according to their culture and tradition. However, that was not what God had planned.

Then Jacob came along. And when it came time to bless the children, he did what God wanted and blessed Ephraim, the younger brother, rather than Manasseh, the oldest, ignoring Joseph's correction.

Rebekah took matters into her own hands because Isaac tried to do the traditional ritual. The blessing was especially important because it was a continuation of the family heritage. And Rebekah protected the family heritage and Isaac's seed, becoming the great nation we have today.

When Rebekah was picked to be Isaac's wife, God knew Rebekah would honor and protect her husband. Esau didn't care about his birthright or the blessing. He showed it in his actions when he sold out his birthright for a bowl of stew. Furthermore, he didn't care who he was going to marry because he ended up marrying Ishmael's daughter.

Rebekah watched carefully what her sons were doing before the eyes of God. When she was pregnant, the two brothers were already fighting and hadn't even been born yet. Rebekah was in tune with God when she inquired of the Lord what was going on in her womb. There were no obstetricians or ultrasounds in those days, which could have revealed what God told her next.

God told her who she was giving birth to, how she would give birth, and what their future would be.

> Isaac prayed to the Lord for his wife because she was childless. The Lord answered his prayer, and his wife Rebekah became pregnant. When the children inside her were struggling with each other, she said, 'If it's like this now, what will become of me?' So, she went to ask the Lord. The Lord said to her, 'Two countries are in your womb. Two nations will go their separate ways from birth. One nation will be stronger than the other, and the older will serve the younger.' When the time came for her to give birth, she had twins. The first one born was red. His whole body was covered with hair, so they named him Esau [Hairy]. Afterwards, his brother was born with his hand holding on to Esau's heel, and

so he was named Jacob [Heel]. Isaac was 60 years old when they were born.

— GENESIS 25:21-26

Note the prophetic word God gave Rebekah. With a word like that, of course, she would have told her husband.

Can you imagine what Rebekah must have thought and felt at that moment? I know exactly where I was when God told me He would give me a child—both Justin and Ellianna. The first time it was a hot summer night, and I was jogging down a hill. The second time He told me He would give me a child, I was driving down the street on a spring afternoon which happened to be Good Friday. I can't tell you how excited I was to receive those prophetic words. And like Rebekah, God told me what my children's future would be. Because it happened to me, I am sure Rebekah was looking to see how the prophecy would play itself out in the lives of her sons.

The time arrived for the blessing to be bestowed, and Isaac was about to make the biggest mistake because he was going to follow tradition.

> When Isaac was old and going blind, he called his older
>   son Esau and said to him, 'Son!' Esau answered, 'Here I
>   am.' Isaac said, 'I'm old. I don't know when I'm going to
>   die. Now take your hunting equipment, your quiver
>   and bow, and go out into the open country and hunt
>   some wild game for me. Prepare a good-tasting meal
>   for me, just the way I like it. Bring it to me to eat so that
>   I will bless you before I die.'

— GENESIS 27:1-2

Isaac and Rebekah were not happy. They were disappointed with the choices Esau made in life. Esau was not following God. And yet Isaac was going to bestow the blessing on him.

This prompted Rebekah to take matters into her hands which caused her to be deceitful. Rather than consulting God as to what she should do, as she did when she was pregnant, she decided to take matters into her own hands. In doing so, she showed her impatience and was happy with the injustice she carried out.

Her deceitful act is a double-edged sword. While Rebekah was protecting the family lineage to make sure Isaac's seed was protected, her actions were a deception.

Why was it so easy for Rebekah to lie and manipulate? Probably because it was practiced in their marriage.

> So Isaac lived in Gerar. When the men of that place asked about his wife, Isaac answered, 'She's my sister.' He was afraid to say 'my wife.' He thought that the men of that place would kill him to get Rebekah, because she was an attractive woman. When he had been there a long time, King Abimelech of the Philistines looked out of his window and saw Isaac caressing his wife Rebekah. Abimelech called for Isaac and said, 'So she's really your wife! How could you say, 'She's my sister'?' Isaac answered him, 'I thought I would be killed because of her.' Then Abimelech said, 'What have you done to us! One of the people might have easily gone to bed with your wife, and then you would have made us guilty of sin. So Abimelech ordered his people, 'Anyone who touches this man or his wife will be put to death.'

> — GENESIS 26:6-11

Here we see a pattern. Isaac's father, Abraham, did the same thing with Sarah as we read about in the previous chapter. Except Sarah was actually Abraham's sister. They told only half the truth, which is still a lie. Now we see the lie and deception in the second and third generations.

We have to break the generational curses within the family line. You have two imperfect people raised two different ways with two different cultures coming together. And with that, you also have personal family traditions within that culture. This is the reason why you need to break the generational curses that have been in your family line.

We know Rebekah did right in getting Jacob the blessing. Isaac didn't reprimand his wife. He didn't get angry at all. At the time, Isaac gave the blessing to Jacob and the curse to Esau, Esau was sobbing, asking if there was any more blessing left for him. But there was no more blessing left supposedly. (Do you understand why I point out lying is practiced in the family?).

Adding to this, Isaac lied to Esau about a second blessing.

> Isaac called for Jacob and blessed him. Then he
> commanded him, 'You are not to marry any of the
> Canaanite women. Quick! Go to Paddan Aram. Go to
> the home of Bethuel, your mother's father, and get
> yourself a wife from there from the daughters of your
> uncle Laban. May God Almighty bless you, make you
> fertile, and increase the number of your descendants so
> that you will become a community of people. May he
> give to you and your descendants the blessing of
> Abraham so that you may take possession of the land
> where you are now living, the land that God gave to

Abraham.' Isaac sent Jacob to Paddan Aram. Jacob
went to live with Laban, son of Bethuel the Aramean
and brother of Rebekah. She was the mother of Jacob
and Esau. Esau learned that Isaac had blessed Jacob
and had sent him away to Paddan Aram to get a wife
from there. He learned that Isaac had blessed Jacob
and had commanded him not to marry any of the
Canaanite women. He also learned that Jacob had
obeyed his father and mother and had left for Paddan
Aram. Esau realized that his father Isaac disapproved
of Canaanite women. So he went to Ishmael and
married Mahalath, daughter of Abraham's son Ishmael
and sister of Nebaioth, in addition to the wives he had.

— GENESIS 28:1-9

Catch this important truth: Rebekah protected Isaac. She didn't
disparage her husband. Isaac, realizing the mistake he almost
made, went to Jacob himself and gave Jacob a second blessing with
specific instructions for Jacob to fulfill the blessing.

This shows love, honor, respect, kindness, and humility on Isaac's
part. He honored the wishes of his wife by listening to her.

Rebekah said to Isaac, 'I can't stand Hittite women! If Jacob
marries a Hittite woman like one of those from around
here, I might as well die.'" As we know, Isaac gave Jacob
another blessing as shown to us in Genesis 28:1-2 (GW),
"Isaac called for Jacob and blessed him. Then he
commanded him, "You are not to marry any of the
Canaanite women. Quick! Go to Paddan Aram. Go to
the home of Bethuel, your mother's father, and get

yourself a wife from there from the daughters of your
uncle Laban.

— GENESIS 27:46

There was another incident in Isaac's family with Abraham and
Sarah when Sarah told Abraham to send away Hagar and his son,
Ishmael. Abraham had respected Sarah's wishes. And now we see
Isaac realizing the truth of what Rebekah did and acting accord-
ingly by sending Jacob to Paddan Aram to find a wife.

Ladies, understand clearly. When you do everything in your
power to protect your man in a godly manner, your man is taking
good note. He will repay you accordingly by granting your
wishes.

Men, when you find a woman who stands by you and defends you,
you have found gold.

Isaac strikes me as a man of honor, integrity, and character. Before
marrying Rebekah, he trusted God to bring him the wife he
needed to have by his side. His strength to honor and cherish her
is evident throughout their marriage. The moment he saw her, he
loved and treated her kindly.

Isaac took her into his mother Sarah's tent. He married
Rebekah. She became his wife, and he loved her. So
Isaac was comforted after his mother's death.

— GENESIS 24:67

Unlike Ishmael, who was married to more than just one woman,
Isaac remained faithful to one woman. Isaac and Rebekah's

marriage was truly a marriage made in Heaven, remaining faithful and enduring everything.

When God chooses your mate, there is peace and unity even though you have trials or disagreements. You will see 1 Corinthians 13, the Love Chapter, played out in that peace and unity.

CHAPTER 4

JACOB AND RACHEL

The love story of Jacob and Rachel is so beautiful. This man worked 14 years of hard labor for his wife's hand in marriage. What guy would do that? Jacob did. Jacob ran away from his hometown after he stole the blessing from his brother Esau. Jacob's parents, Rebekah and Isaac, told him to go to his mother's hometown and look for her brother, Laban (his uncle). Let's read of his arrival.

> Jacob continued on his trip and came to the land in the east. He looked around, and out in a field he saw a well with a large stone over the opening. Three flocks of sheep were lying down near it, because the flocks were watered from that well. When all the flocks were gathered there, the stone would be rolled off the opening of the well so that the sheep could be watered. Then the stone would be put back in place over the opening of the well. Jacob asked some people, 'My friends, where are you from?' 'We're from Haran,' they replied. He asked them, 'Do you know Laban, Nahor's grandson?'

They answered, 'We do.' 'How is he doing?' Jacob asked
them. 'He's fine,' they answered. 'Here comes his
daughter Rachel with the sheep.' 'It's still the middle of
the day,' he said. 'It isn't time yet to gather the livestock.
Water the sheep. Then let them graze.' They replied,
'We can't until all the flocks are gathered. When the
stone is rolled off the opening of the well, we can water
the sheep.' While he was still talking to them, Rachel
arrived with her father's sheep, because she was a shep-
herd. Jacob saw Rachel, daughter of his Uncle Laban,
with his uncle Laban's sheep. He came forward and
rolled the stone off the opening of the well and watered
his uncle Laban's sheep. Then Jacob kissed Rachel and
sobbed loudly. When Jacob told Rachel that he was her
father's nephew and that he was Rebekah's son, she ran
and told her father. As soon as Laban heard the news
about his sister's son Jacob, he ran to meet him. He
hugged and kissed him and brought him into his home.
Then Jacob told Laban all that had happened. Laban
said to him, 'You are my own flesh and blood.'

— GENESIS 29:1-14

I find this setting interesting. There was another woman, many
years before, going to the well to feed the sheep. That woman was
Jacob's mother, Rebekah, as we read in the previous love story.

Here we find Jacob at the well, most likely the same one. For
Rachel, it was just another ordinary day. She led the sheep to
water as she was a shepherdess just like her aunt, Jacob's mother,
Rebekah. Although it was customary in those days for the young
women to go to the well to draw their water, the young men would

be there too. It was a great way to meet a young woman for marriage.

Something amazing took place at this well. As Jacob was inquiring about his Uncle Laban, the men told him, *"Here comes Rachel, his daughter."* It is a very sure bet to say, "Love at first sight." He continued to ask why they were coming so early to water the sheep. You see, in those days, water was scarce, and it had to be protected by those who owned it. Therefore, a big rock was placed on top the well requiring all of the shepherds to work together to roll it away. Rachel had arrived and was waiting for the rest of the shepherds to arrive. Jacob showed his strength by going to her and rolling this big, huge rock away to help her water the sheep. Can you imagine Rachel's delight? Talk about Mr. Muscleman!

We shouldn't be shocked at his amazing strength. After all, he was his mother's son. We remember the strength it must have taken for his mother to water the camels when his grandfather's servant arrived at the same place and met his mother. He had been brought up by a mother who wasn't afraid of hard work.

Every woman wants a man with great strength, resilience, power, and character. This is exactly what Rachel saw that day. Let me just say, as a woman, I admire this about a man.

It is not just about finding a man that can provide for us. It is about his character. He saw a need, and he took control. He made something happen by himself.

Imagine this: Rachel just got there, in the middle of the day after working so hard to keep the sheep from straying away and protecting them from wild animals. This was not an easy job. It was not for the faint of heart. She was tired, and she had to wait for the rest to show up to roll that heavy rock away. Jacob steps up to the plate and removes it, making her life easy.

Ladies, please hear me loud and clear. We might not like our man working so hard. But he is just doing what needs to be done so that our life is much easier.

Personally, I respect and admire a man that works hard for his family. A hard-working man needs to be respected, celebrated, encouraged and praised. Complaining about his work ethic displays the wrong kind of spirit.

I understand that some men might be workaholics. And, if that is the case, then find gentle ways to remind him that you want him, not his money, possessions, or extra things. Never make him feel bad about his work ethic. This is who God made man to be. *"You will work by the sweat of your brow."* Remember that before you complain.

This might not be the most popular thing to say, but it is the truth. As women, we must appreciate our husbands for the love they provide for their families.

Rachel showed her humility, and the Bible describes her as a beautiful woman. It says, *"Rachel was lovely in form and beautiful."* In other words, she didn't mind getting her hands dirty.

Have you ever been around sheep? I have. My parents had sheep as pets. We had several of them. When I visited my parents, I would have to change my shoes and clothes to go see them. It is not a glamorous job.

Her beauty far surpassed what she must have looked like after being in the field watching over her flock. Jacob went over and kissed her. Now, it wasn't a passionate kiss, but a kiss of greeting as he tells her he is her relative.

What happens next is amazing.

> Jacob stayed with him for a whole month. Then Laban said to him, 'Just because you're my relative doesn't mean that you should work for nothing. Tell me what your wages should be.' Laban had two daughters. The name of the older one was Leah, and the name of the younger one was Rachel. Leah had attractive eyes, but Rachel had a beautiful figure and beautiful features. Jacob loved Rachel. So he offered, 'I'll work seven years in return for your younger daughter Rachel.' Laban responded, 'It's better that I give her to you than to any other man. Stay with me.' Jacob worked seven years in return for Rachel, but the years seemed like only a few days to him because he loved her.
>
> — GENESIS 29:14-20

Jacob's work ethic continues. He was there for only a month but worked hard. Laban recognized this about Jacob and asked him, *"What are your wages?"* His response is astonishing to me. He didn't ask for sheep, money, or possessions. He asked for Rachel's hand in marriage, the woman he loved.

Imagine, *"I will work seven years for your daughter Rachel."* Call me sappy, but I love this. The man didn't care how hard he had to work to get this woman. When you are looking at real love, look no further.

Take notice of what he says, *"The years seemed like only a few days to him because he loved her."* Ok, I want this. This is the kind of love that we should want and the kind of man we should choose. A man who loves you so much that he doesn't care how hard he has to work to win your heart.

It wasn't superficial for Jacob. It was genuine, sincere, truthful, and real love. Men who want to work hard to provide for their wives are rare and priceless. Please understand this clearly.

> At the end of the seven years Jacob said to Laban, 'The time is up; give me my wife! I want to sleep with her.' So Laban invited all the people of that place and gave a wedding feast. In the evening he took his daughter Leah and brought her to Jacob. Jacob slept with her. When morning came, he realized it was Leah. (Laban had given his slave Zilpah to his daughter Leah as her slave.)
>
> — GENESIS 29:21-24

Part of me feels sorry for Leah and the other part of me doesn't feel sorry for her. Let me explain. Leah and everyone around them knew the love Jacob had for Rachel. That is very clear. We also know from the account of her Aunt Rebekah, Laban asked Rebekah if she wanted to marry Isaac and even asked how long she wanted to remain at home before making her journey. Therefore, we shouldn't assume Laban made Leah agree to marry Jacob.

Leah was not forced to marry Jacob. Leah could have spoken up and avoided a loveless marriage. Leah even accused Rachel, when Rachel wanted the mandrakes, *"Isn't it enough you have stolen the love of my husband? You want my mandrakes too!"* What an interesting statement to make.

Rachel didn't steal anything. Rachel was promised to Jacob. It was Leah who went ahead with a terrible plan to catch a man. Please note that a woman sleeping with a man and bearing him children will not cause a man to love her as in this case.

Imagine what it must have been like for both Jacob and Rachel the day the seven years ended. Jacob could not have been more explicit about his love or intentions towards Rachel. He worked and waited seven years. Can you imagine the love he had for her? Now it was time for him to take his bride, share his life with her, and show her his love.

God created sex. Sex is between a man and a woman within the context of marriage. We live in a world where anything goes but, the Bible is clear on this matter.

> Marriage should be honored by all and the marriage bed
> kept undefiled, for God will judge the sexually immoral
> and adulterers.
>
> — HEBREWS 13:4

We have allowed the world to cheapen this amazing gift God has given us.

One-night stands are not genuine love. It is not real. It is a cheap imitation of the greatest gift of all.

We read in 1 Corinthians 13, *"And the greatest of this is love."* Affairs with married people are not love. God does not bring married people to single people.

Marriage is sacred. We need to respect and honor the people with whom we come in contact who are married to someone else. Please hear me. God will never bless anyone who steals another person's spouse.

We need not look further than King David, who had sex with Bathsheba. The prophet Nathan came to him and condemned him. That sin was deadly. It cost David the life of their first child. The child died.

God has not changed His mind on this sin of sexual immorality. It is not that God kills you or your child. It is a sin that is committed against our own bodies.

> Stay away from sexual sins. Other sins that people commit
> don't affect their bodies the same way sexual sins do.
> People who sin sexually sin against their own bodies.
>
> — CORINTHIANS 6:18

God has dedicated an entire book, "Song of Solomon" to describe this beautiful gift of sex between a husband and wife. You can't read Song of Solomon without genuinely feeling the purest form of love expressed by the act of intimacy. Determine in your heart that you will not allow yourself to be defiled in such a way and you will not pursue or chase a married person. It is a sin. God holds us responsible for our actions.

We know right from wrong, and we are expected to do what is right. Any form of sexual sin is sinning against yourself and is a selfish kind of love, as we discussed in Chapter 1.

In those days marriage wasn't like it is now. There was a wedding. But the men stayed with the men and the women with the women.

The parents would bring the wife at the end to her husband, which is what took place here. Most likely, drinking would have taken place. And in the darkness of the night, Jacob wouldn't have noticed what took place until morning. Let's look at the account given to us.

> That's what Jacob did. He finished the week with Leah. Then Laban gave his daughter Rachel to him as his wife. (Laban had given his slave Bilhah to his daughter Rachel as her slave.) Jacob slept with Rachel too. He loved Rachel more than Leah, and he worked for Laban another seven years.
>
> — GENESIS 29:25-30

What a terrible tragedy. He had been deceived. Laban tells him to finish his honeymoon week with Leah, and he would be given Rachel to be his wife. However, he had to work for another seven years.

Jacob could have refused. He could have said forget it. But that burning love he had for Rachel would not allow him to give up on her. Can you say, "Real and genuine love?"

I don't want to ignore Leah. I feel very sorry for Leah. Leah was never loved by Jacob. I want to insert this here because perhaps you have been married to someone who never loved you and doesn't love you. God saw Leah wasn't loved, and He opened her womb to bare 10 sons for Jacob as well as one daughter.

In those days, it was a huge honor to bear sons for your husband. God gave her ten of them. But her pain was real.

If you are in a loveless marriage, I don't pretend to have any answers here. However, I will say, "God sees, and God will avenge you." Hold on to God and pray God will restore, heal, and bind up the brokenness in your marriage or remove you from it. Do not take matters into your own hands. Trust and be led of God. He will avenge you. God will not fail you. As He saw Leah, He will see you and provide a way for you too.

Jacob and Rachel did not have a fairytale marriage.

Rachel was jealous of Leah for having children, while she was barren. In fact, she complained to Jacob about it. We see there was a fight. Rachel saw that she could not have children for Jacob, and she became jealous of her sister. She said to Jacob, "Give me children, or I'll die!" Jacob became angry with Rachel and asked, "Can I take the place of God, who has kept you from having children?" (See Genesis 30:1-2)

Rachel asked something of Jacob that he could not do. Rachel was well aware Jacob loved her and not Leah. Yet, she wanted something from her husband he didn't have the power to give.

How many times do we make demands of our spouse for something they cannot give? Is it possible that our demands of our spouses are our own selfish desires? Are we asking our spouses to do things that are impossible for them to do?

Some things are out of their control. This is where we become mean-spirited. Nothing good comes out of selfishness. I have seen way too many couples destroy their marriage because of selfish attitudes, ambitions, and wrong thinking.

Look at 1 Corinthians 13 again and meditate on these things so we do not destroy our own marriages. A smart woman builds her house while the other one tears it down.

This applies to men as well. A smart man or woman will do all they can to build up and not tear down. This is the foundation of the basis of love and marriage, to build each other up, to support each other, being proud and encouraging, not acting as Rachel did.

Then Rachel makes another mistake.

> She said, 'Here's my servant Bilhah. Sleep with her. She can have children for me, and I can build a family for myself through her.' So she gave him her slave Bilhah as his wife, and Jacob slept with her. Bilhah became pregnant, and she gave birth to a son for Jacob. Rachel said, 'Now God has judged in my favor. He has heard my prayer and has given me a son.'" So she named him Dan [He Judges]. Rachel's slave Bilhah became pregnant again and gave birth to a second son for Jacob. Rachel said, 'I have had a great struggle with my sister, and I have won!' So she named him Naphtali [My Struggle].
>
> — GENESIS 30:3-8

Although it was customary to do so, she took matters into her own hands, like Sarah, Jacob's grandmother. How sad. He learned nothing from the past.

Leah was now in on the act, too. She wasn't satisfied with the children she already gave him. She told Jacob to go and sleep with her maidservant too.

Honestly, I can't even believe this story. It started as the most amazing love story of all love stories and ends up turning ugly.

Jacob doesn't deny them. He did as they asked. Jacob never loved those maidservants. They were used.

Ladies, I added this in the story to make a strong point. Sorry to the men, but it is true. A man is wired differently than a woman. A man can just get intimate without loving the woman. Please see what I see here. Imagine being in a situation such as this; enough to get pregnant and then left. While these women lived as Jacob's servants, they never received the same acclamation as Jacob's wives, Leah and Rachel.

God was good to Rachel, as we see here:

> Then God remembered Rachel. God answered her prayer
> and made it possible for her to have children. So she
> became pregnant and gave birth to a son. Then she
> said, 'God has taken away my disgrace.' She named him
> Joseph [May He Give Another] and said, 'May the Lord
> give me another son.'
>
> — GENESIS 30:22-24

Imagine if Rachel had just waited for God to answer her. We make grave mistakes when we take matters into our own hands.

This story has a sad ending.

> When they were still some distance from Ephrath, Rachel
> went into labor and was having severe labor pains.
> During one of her pains, the midwife said to her, 'Don't
> be afraid! You're having another son!' Rachel was dying.
> As she took her last breath, she named her son Benoni
> [Son of My Sorrow], but his father named him

Benjamin [Son of My Right Hand]. Rachel died and
was buried on the way to Ephrath (that is, Bethlehem).
Then Jacob set up a stone as a marker for her grave.
The same marker is at Rachel's grave today.

— GENESIS 35:16-18

What started as an amazing love story ends with Rachel dying at
an early age, giving birth to another son. Rachel's grave is still
there today.

God knew Jacob was deceived. You see, God saw Jacob's intent was
not to have two wives. His love was always for Rachel.

Jacob loved Rachel for the rest of his days. How do we know?
Because Jacob protected Joseph and Benjamin more than the rest
of his sons. So much so that the Bible says, *"Jacob made a special
coat of many colors for Joseph."* As we know, Joseph was hated by his
ten brothers. All because of the love Jacob had for Rachel.

Real love never dies. It overcomes all obstacles, and it endures
until the very end.

There are so many lessons in this story. It starts with such pure
love, affection, endurance, winning against all odds. Are you
hearing me? Work hard to endure in the worst of times.

Love wins all the time. It can't be beaten when we follow the will
of God. It does not cheat, and it is not to be given away to just
anyone.

Real love is worth waiting for. Wait for God's timing. And when it
comes, protect it with everything you have.

Discussion For Couples and Groups:

Rachel's Strengths	Rachel's Weaknesses
Kind (Genesis 29:9)	Rude (Genesis 31:17-31)
	Deceitful (Genesis 31:19)

Jacob's Strengths	Jacob's Weaknesses
Patient (Genesis 29:14-18)	Deceitful (Genesis 31: 20-29)
	Selfish (Genesis 31:17-31)

The world doesn't understand the most used word "love." The word "love" is used frivolously with phrases like "I love fishing" or "I love chocolate."

In this story, with all the conniving, lying and cheating that was going on with Jacob, this man loved and adored Rachel. Rachel was his everything. He overlooked many things about Rachel as we will be discussing.

Who doesn't want a man who loves her as much as this man loved Rachel? Hello! I'm raising both my hands right here.

I don't believe Rachel truly and fully loved Jacob.

It all began when she went to him and said...

'Give me children, or I'll die!'

— GENESIS 3:1

Rachel never appreciated or respected the love her husband had for her. Rachel knew it was her that her husband desired and truly loved. After all, he had worked 14 years for her father, Laban, to have her as his wife.

I ask this question of every woman, "Shouldn't a man who works 14 years to marry you deserve your undying respect and admiration?" If that is not proof of love, I don't know what is.

And to men, "Don't you want a woman, who after you have worked so hard to get as your wife, wants to be there as your helpmate?"

What does it mean to be a helpmate? It means she will come alongside you, supporting and encouraging you in all your endeavors in whatever God has called you to do.

There is a saying that states, "Behind every great man, there is a great woman." This doesn't mean the woman is greater than the man. It is because she has caught your vision. She knows what God has called you to do and prepared you to be. She is not afraid to roll up her sleeves and work towards ensuring that the dreams and visions God has placed in your heart will come to pass. She is building her house on a solid rock to stand. If the royal priesthood as the husband succeeds, she becomes blessed and happy with the fruit of her hands. Ladies, you better get this right. If you want a happy husband and not a sorrowful one, you better understand this concept and put it into practice.

Men, there are some women that, no matter what you do, are just not going to appreciate you. In this case, Rachel wanted a child; she was jealous of Leah and placed an unrealistic expectation on her husband as if he were God and could give her a child.

When she saw he couldn't, that it was not Jacob who gave life, she quickly handed over her servant to Jacob, causing a ripple effect and allowing Leah to do the same with her servant. What a mess!

When that was still not good enough for Rachel, she decided to exchange Leah's mandrakes. The mandrakes were flowers that also produced some fruit. And according to tradition, it was said the mandrakes represent fertility. So, if you had mandrakes, it would mean you would become pregnant. This tradition of mandrakes was ungodly and a form of witchcraft.

God had already made a promise that Jacob would be the father of 12 tribes. He did not need witchcraft or any other satanic way of bringing that about. Where was Rachel's faith in God to do as He promised?

First, we see the idols that clearly proved she believed in idol worship. Now we see the mandrakes that had superstitious meaning, basically a form of divination.

Jacob already knew what God was calling him to. I don't see Rachel in any way being a part of his calling. Let me be direct: Men, you better be very, very sure that the woman you marry is the one God has chosen for your life because your calling and your future depends on it. The dreams and visions God has placed within you will either come forth or die, bringing joy or sorrow.

Men, women who live by the Bible clearly acknowledge and understand you are the head; you are the royal priesthood. You were created to lead, so lead well. By committing an ungodly act, Rachel gave her husband up to have relations with another woman, not caring that Jacob neither loved Leah nor cared to be with Leah. She was willing to hurt both her husband and Leah just to get her own selfish and evil way. That night it was Leah who conceived and not Rachel.

Rachel was not serving the same God as Jacob.

...Rachel stole her father's idols.

— GENESIS 31:19

If she were serving the God of Jacob, she would have no purpose for those idols. She was going in a completely different direction. When Laban, her father, accused Jacob of stealing the household gods, Jacob was so sure it wasn't them, he cursed the person who took it. Rachel was not fully surrendered to God because she was an idol worshipper and, from this account, a thief.

You see, Jacob never asked God if Rachel was to be his wife. He loved her, but we don't find where it says that Rachel loved Jacob. Jacob had a mandate from God. But Rachel didn't stand by Jacob in this regard. She was a hindrance to him and his calling.

Finally, God blesses her with a son they called "Joseph." But that still wasn't enough for her. She wanted more. God blessed her with her second child. However, during her labor, she ended up dying, and her last word was the name she chose for her newborn, "Benoni," meaning "son of sorrow." That should tell you where her spiritual life was.

Thank God Jacob stepped up and spoke and renamed him, calling him, "Benjamin," meaning "the son of the right hand."

> Then they moved on from Bethel. When they were still
> some distance from Ephrath, Rachel went into labor
> and was having severe labor pains.

— GENESIS 35:16-18

This story makes me sad because the very thing she wanted was to have children, and she died having the second child.

Jacob was filled with sorrow when Rachel died.

> As I was returning from Paddan, to my sorrow Rachel died in the land of Canaan while we were still on the way, a little distance from Ephrath. So I buried her there beside the road to Ephrath" (that is, Bethlehem).

— GENESIS 48:7

There is another woman in the Bible. Her name is Hannah. Like Rachel, Hannah couldn't have children. Rather than doing things her own way, Hannah knelt down in prayer and sought the Lord on the matter.

The Lord blessed her with Samuel, and she fulfilled her vow to God. Hannah gave Samuel over to the Lord's service. And then God granted her three more sons and two daughters.

Rachel wanted children, and instead of doing it God's way, Rachel took matters into her own hands, giving her husband to the servant.

One woman (Hannah) got to have many children because she did it God's way and got to enjoy her children. The other woman (Rachel) tried to do things her own way. Her focus was all about having children. But she died in childbirth and never got to enjoy her children.

Ladies, do not allow anything to come between you and God or between you and your husband. Get rid of whatever idols and superstitions stop God's blessings in your life and ruin your marriage.

In studying Rachel, I can only find one attribute, and that is her strength. Her strength was kindness. Ironically, her kindness was shown only to animals, not to Jacob. Can you imagine what a marriage they would have had if Rachel had extended kindness to Jacob rather than just the animals?

Through all of this, God still considers her as having helped build the tribes of Israel.

> All the people who were at the gate, including the leaders, said, 'We are witnesses. May the LORD make this wife, who is coming into your home, like Rachel and Leah, both of who built our family of Israel. So show your strength of character in Ephrathah and make a name for yourself in Bethlehem.'
>
> — RUTH 4:11

Jacob, on the other hand, really put into practice 1 Corinthians 13 toward his wife. Even though that marriage caused a lot of heartache and sorrow for him, he loved her unconditionally. He constantly assured her that his heart beat only for her. Joseph and Benjamin became his favorites out of the 12 children he had. His love for Rachel continued even after her death, until the day he died.

Ladies, when you have a man that loves you in this way, you move heaven and earth to keep him happy. And yes, there are men out there like Jacob. God will bring you that man if you are the kind of woman you need to be.

Jacob was a deceiver. His name even means "deceiver." Could it be that the reason Rachel wasn't sure about the God of Jacob was because she knew about how he deceived her father?

> Then Jacob took fresh-cut branches of poplar, almond, and
> plane trees and peeled the bark on them in strips of
> white, uncovering the white which was on the
> branches. He placed the peeled branches in the
> troughs directly in front of the flocks, at the watering
> places where the flocks came to drink. When they were
> in heat and came to drink, they mated in front of the
> branches. Then they gave birth to young that were
> striped, speckled, or spotted. Jacob separated the rams
> from the flock and made the rest of the sheep face any
> that were striped or black in Laban's flocks. So he made
> separate herds for himself and did not add them to
> Laban's flocks. Whenever the stronger of the flocks
> were in heat, Jacob would lay the branches in the
> troughs in front of them so that they would mate by the
> branches. But when the flocks in heat were weak, he
> didn't lay down the branches. So the weaker ones
> belonged to Laban and the stronger ones to Jacob. As a
> result, Jacob became very wealthy. He had large flocks,
> male and female slaves, camels, and donkeys.
>
> — GENESIS 35:37-43

Jacob's biggest failure was deception, and deception came easy for him. Men, may I humbly say that, as the royal priesthood for your home, you are setting an example before your wife and your children? Jacob learned from his mother about deception and copied her. His father was also deceptive, and Jacob learned from him too.

Isaac learned how to be deceptive from Abraham. Do you now fully comprehend that the sins of the father fell into each generation?

Jacob's sons were also deceivers.

> So they took Joseph's robe, killed a goat, and dipped the
> robe in the blood. Then they brought the special robe
> with long sleeves to their father and said, 'We found
> this. You better examine it to see whether it's your son's
> robe or not.' He recognized it and said, 'It is my son's
> robe! A wild animal has eaten him! Joseph must have
> been torn to pieces!'
>
> — GENESIS 37:31-33

In the previous chapter I spoke regarding generational curses. We, as the children of God, are the royal priesthood. However, God has given the role of priesthood to the man in his household. This means he must demonstrate to his wife and children a life lived out for God in obedience to the Word of God, showing character, honor, integrity, and all forms of godliness.

It is also his job to tear down generational curses. Obviously, the family suffered from deception. Jacob continued to allow it to happen in his life and opened the door for him to be deceived by his father-in-law. That's how he ended up with Leah. Rachel, Leah, and his children were all watching the deceptive plans.

Men, catch this and ponder on it. Are you living your life before God first, your wife second, and your children third? Because what you do will affect the kind of marriage you have and the kind of marriage your children will have.

In all of this, this man genuinely loved his wife. There is nothing at all in his entire marriage to cause Rachel to believe she wasn't loved. I truly admire Jacob. No wonder God set him apart and changed his name from Jacob to Israel and brought him forth to become a great nation. Men can learn from this kind of love.

Be the priest of your home and God will grant you the desires of your heart according to His will. It is your responsibility, Men of God, to operate your home in the godly way, tearing down any known or unknown generational sin in your family and that of your wife's family. When looking for a wife for life, ask for the will of God to be done and choose a wife like Sarah or Rebekah. Rachel just didn't have what it took to be a godly wife and to assist Jacob in the calling God had for him.

CHAPTER 5

KING ARTAXERXES & QUEEN ESTHER

The story of Queen Esther and King Artaxerxes is unique among all other love stories in the Bible. God is doing something completely different in bringing these two people together for marriage.

King Artaxerxes put away his wife, Queen Vashti, and replaced her with Queen Esther. It's interesting that God took a divorced man and put him with a godly young woman who was a virgin.

I love Queen Esther's story because God can create an amazing love story regardless of where people are in life. King Artaxerxes was a broken man, humiliated before his staff and colleagues and in his kingdom. Queen Vashti was disrespectful, rude, and dishonorable.

The worst thing a woman can do is demonstrate a lack of admiration and honor towards her husband in the company of others. King Artaxerxes did not ask her to do what was not common. He wanted to showcase her as the Queen and his wife before the officials in attendance at the great banquet.

> On the seventh day when the king was drunk on wine, he
> ordered Mehuman, Biztha, Harbona, Bigtha, Abagtha,
> Zethar, and Carcas, the seven eunuchs who served
> under King Xerxes, to bring Queen Vashti in front of
> the king, wearing her royal crown. He wanted to show
> the people, especially the officials, her beauty, because
> she was very attractive. But Queen Vashti refused the
> king's command that the eunuchs delivered to her. As a
> result, the king became very angry, and his rage burned
> inside him.
>
> — ESTHER 1:10-12

There comes a point in time when a spouse is dishonored and disrespected so much that love is eroded. In this case, Queen Vashti had humiliated her husband before the entire kingdom. There was no going back for her.

You should never dishonor, disrespect, or humiliate your spouse in any way, shape, or form, whether you are the husband or the wife. It leads to a disastrous situation like it did with Queen Vashti. God always honors the one who has been wronged.

King Artaxerxes became more than just angry. His rage burned inside of him, and he had every right to be enraged. The Queen had set a terrible example of how a woman should treat her husband as well as her title.

For example, we don't hold beauty pageants to pick the most beautiful woman in the world. After all, not every beautiful woman in the world is competing for that title. However, the winner of a pageant will be representing the sponsors as well as the host. So, whenever they call upon her to carry out a task, she can't say she won't be there. She must be there. The whole point is to showcase the most beautiful woman in the world. People are going to the event because they want to see her.

Due to Vashti's inappropriate behavior, she was banished from King Artaxerxes' presence, lost her title, and was never called by the King again.

> If it pleases you, Your Majesty, issue a royal decree. It should be recorded in the decrees of the Persians and Medes, never to be repealed, that Vashti may never again appear in front of King Xerxes. Furthermore, Your Majesty, you should give her royal position to another woman who is more worthy than she.
>
> — ESTHER 1:19

What an embarrassing moment for a woman who had beauty but no honor.

King Artaxerxes was angry with Vashti for refusing his request, and as a result, he called forth his advisers.

> Now, the king usually asked for advice from all the experts in royal decrees and decisions, from those closest to him—Carshena, Shethar, Admatha, Tarshish, Meres, Marsena, and Memucan. These seven officials of the Persians and Medes had access to the king and held the highest rank in the kingdom. The king asked these wise men who knew the times, 'According to the royal decrees, what must we do with Queen Vashti since she did not obey King Xerxes' command, which the eunuchs delivered?'

— ESTHER 1:13-15

It's always a bad idea to treat your spouse with wrong attitudes and emotions in public. And let me say this, we all have our breaking points. The best thing any person can do is control their emotions and not strike back, even in private. There are actions, ideas, and thoughts toward a person's spouse that should never cross a person's mind.

As the story continues, King Artaxerxes regretted banishing Vashti.

> Later, when King Xerxes got over his raging anger, he remembered Vashti, what she had done, and what had been decided against her.

— ESTHER 2:1

Actions lead to problems when left unchecked. Now you see the damage caused by Vashti's behavior. She did something she should not have done, then King Artaxerxes got angry. There were others involved who influenced a negative decision, which caused Vashti to be banished from the king's presence. When we behave in an ungodly manner before others, they often lose respect for us too.

How you treat your spouse in public or at family gatherings will either reflect badly on you or bring you and your spouse honor. Bring honor to yourself and your spouse by doing what is right.

King Artaxerxes was now depressed. He regretted the decision he had made. This is what happens when there is such anger towards the person who has done the unthinkable. King Artaxerxes made a hasty decision, never mind that he was intoxicated. He made a terrible decision in the heat of emotions. He was a hot-tempered man, and it showed when he discussed his wife with the kingdom officials by asking their opinion as to what he should do. It ended their marriage.

After all of this, a young woman named Hadassah, a pure young woman, is brought to King Artaxerxes.

> So the king's personal staff said to him, 'Search for attractive young virgins for the king. And appoint scouts in all the provinces of your kingdom to gather all the attractive young virgins and bring them to the fortress of Susa, to the women's quarters. There, in the care of the king's eunuch Hegai, the guardian of the women, they will have their beauty treatment. Then the young woman who pleases you, Your Majesty, will become queen instead of Vashti.'
>
> — ESTHER 2:2-4

Here is where God makes everything beautiful in His time. In the citadel of Susa, there was a beautiful young woman named Hadassah. She was being brought up by her Uncle Mordecai. The King's men brought Hadassah to the citadel of Susa and placed her under the care of Hegai.

Hadassah was not only beautiful, but she also possessed the finest of attributes; respectful, kind, gentle, humble, honorable, and she knew her place. This won the attention of Hegai, and he favored her. He moved Hadassah and her attendants into the best place in the harem. Hadassah had listened to the counsel of Mordecai, who had taught her to be a godly young woman

It is important to know and understand that receiving godly counsel is the greatest attribute a man or woman can possess. Great men and women are made when they are moldable and teachable. Those who choose to remain unteachable and refuse to take wise, godly counsel will never accomplish anything, and they will fall.

King Artaxerxes would ask for a young woman and spend the night with her. Then he would decide if she would be his queen. Part of the beauty treatments also meant Hadassah would be given a Persian name. Her new name was now Esther.

When it came time for Esther to appear before the King, Esther asked the King's eunuch for his opinion on what to wear, and Esther was taken to the King who was in the royal residence.

> Now, the king loved Esther more than all the other women
> and favored her over all the other virgins...
>
> — ESTHER 2:17

Right here is where she makes her most brilliant move. Esther left it to Hegai to choose what she would wear.

As a woman, I have my own look. I know what looks good on me and what doesn't look good on me. When I am going to an important party or meeting, I try on tons of outfits before making my final decision. I don't trust anybody with how I am going to look. I have a mirror, and I know what look I'm trying to achieve. So, I don't leave it to anyone else to pick my outfit. Therefore, I must ask myself why Esther would leave this important decision to Hegai.

This decision would either make her queen or keep her enslaved for the rest of her life with no future hope of being loved by another man. She would be confined in the harem for the rest of her life. Prison would have been better than confinement with no future and no hope.

This was a brilliant move on her part. Hegai knew her, and she trusted his opinion. He knew precisely what King Artaxerxes liked and didn't like. In other words, he had dressed other women before her. Every piece of jewelry, gown, shoes, purse, perfume, and make-up, along with hairpieces, was available. She could have had a field day.

Instead, she wisely asked, "What do you suggest I wear?" That question and the answer became her wedding ticket. The moral to the story: Know what your partner likes and what pleases only their eyes.

King Artaxerxes was a beaten, depressed, and hurt man. Esther's beautiful appearance and demeanor—respectful, kind, humble, honorable, loving, and caring way—touched the man's heart.

> Now, the king loved Esther more than all the other women and favored her over all the other virgins. So he put the royal crown on her head and made her queen instead of Vashti. Then the king held a great banquet for Esther. He invited all his officials and his advisers. He also declared that day a holiday in the provinces, and he handed out gifts from his royal generosity.
>
> — ESTHER 2:17-18

Notice the time of mourning has ended. The last banquet with the previous queen was heartbreaking, and it spiraled down to the end of a marriage and the end of a queen. Four years later, God intervened and brought a new queen to the palace, Queen Esther, for such a time as this. It was a day of celebration and honor, and that day was proclaimed a holiday.

I love the way God ends love stories.

The Word of God says that gifts were distributed with royal liberality, meaning nothing was spared. It was a real celebration and restoration for a man who had been dishonored and humiliated. God had brought him an awesome, honorable, and beautiful new queen.

This is how God restores. He restores better than before, and He does it tremendously. This should bring hope to anyone who has been hurt and destroyed by a previous marriage or relationship. God sees everything, and He restores the broken. It doesn't matter what happened to you. If you are the one who was hurt, God will bring you your king or your queen. Take courage. Your love story isn't finished yet.

The day came when Esther had to appear before King Artaxerxes, without being summoned, to tell him there was a plot to kill her people. She had not been called by the King for 30 days. Anyone that appeared before the King without being summoned could be put to death.

Can you imagine that? If you wanted to see your husband the King, you had to be asked to go to him. But Esther still honored, respected, and loved him. How does Esther handle this situation? She prayed.

> Esther sent this reply back to Mordecai, 'Assemble all the
> Jews in Susa. Fast for me: Do not eat or drink at all for
> three entire days. My servants and I will also fast. After

that, I will go to the king, even if it is against a royal decree. If I die, I die.'

— ESTHER 4:15-16

This was the reason for Queen Esther's success in life and in marriage. I want to point out something very important in the next verse.

Mordecai did just as Esther had commanded him.

— ESTHER 4:17

What a contrast there is between the counsel of Esther to Mordecai versus the counsel given by the King's official to King Artaxerxes. Take this to heart: Never seek the advice of ungodly people.

Note the wisdom of Esther. She didn't go running to the King. The first thing she did was go to inquire of the Lord. She knew that approaching him was breaking the law and knew she could have been killed. She needed the wisdom of God to know when and how to approach her husband.

Ladies, it's not always wise to go running to your husband when there is a difficult situation that he's not ready to hear. One of my favorite Bible verses is...

The king's heart is like streams of water. Both are under the Lord's control. He turns them in any direction he chooses.

— PROVERBS 21:1

Esther knew that only God could change the King's heart for her to see him and for her request to be granted. There is great wisdom in her actions.

After the third day of her fast, Esther put on her royal robes and went to her King. Picture this scene with me: Esther is walking down the hall with her head held high wearing her royal robes to go see the King, her husband, who hasn't summoned her. Going to him without being called could bring about her execution. Imagine what she must have felt and was thinking. Could her husband be with another woman? Would he be angry? Would he sentence her to death? Could he be in a meeting with other officials?

I'm sure what had happened to the previous queen was vivid in her mind. I believe the Spirit of God was upon her after her fast, which caused her to walk down the hall with great confidence in the God wherein she placed her hope, trusting in the love between a husband and wife.

I think about the guards in the hall guarding the King. What were they thinking, knowing the King had not called her? Keep in mind, Esther found favor with everyone in the palace. Now the guards protecting the King see Esther, whom they loved, walking in to see the King who hasn't called her. By law, those guards had the right to kill her before she even reached the door of the King. But, because she was loved by everyone, she made it to the door.

> When the king saw Queen Esther standing in the entrance,
> she won his favor. So the king held out the golden
> scepter that was in his hand to Esther. Esther went up
> to him and touched the top of the scepter.
>
> — ESTHER 5:2

Once again, Esther shows great respect by going to him and touching the top of the scepter, recognizing him as her authority. Notice that she said nothing.

She doesn't blurt out anything, showing the King respect and honor by waiting for him to address her. This scene is astonishing and baffling. Let me explain. King Artaxerxes made a big deal about the disrespectful attitude Queen Vashti displayed. Everyone in the kingdom knew what took place, including the guards.

What changed for King Artaxerxes? He knew this queen stood by him, admired him, respected him, protected him, and loved him. And this is how I know King Artaxerxes loved Esther; he wasn't angry for her taking the initiative to come see him. He didn't display any anger, frustration, or impatience.

> Then the king asked her, "What is troubling you, Queen Esther? What would you like? Even if it is up to half of the kingdom, it will be granted to you."
>
> — ESTHER 5:3

Wow! A man completely in love with his wife. There's no question.

Ladies, treat your husband as the authority and respect him in the marriage.

The King said something awe-inspiring.

> Then the king asked her, 'What is troubling you, Queen Esther? What would you like? Even if it is up to half of the kingdom, it will be granted to you.'
>
> — ESTHER 5:3

Ladies, this shows the great admiration, respect, and honor that a man in love with his wife gives. He was about to give half of everything he owned to her. Esther, being the wise wife and queen, knowing her husband would do what was right, gives the best answer any woman could give. *"If it pleases you, Your Majesty."*

Note what she just said. Esther was willing to please him, but Vashti didn't care about pleasing the King. Vashti was selfish and disrespectful. Esther decides to invite the King and the man who wanted to destroy her people, not just once but twice, to a banquet. At that banquet, Esther made sure every need of her husband was met. There wasn't anything lacking in the banquet room. Esther shined like the brightest star and made no demands.

At the second banquet, Esther's excellence continued to shine. For the second time, we see the King asking Esther about her request.

> On the second day, while they were drinking wine, the king asked Esther, "What is your request, Queen Esther? It will be granted to you. And what would you like? Even if it is up to half of the kingdom, it will be granted.
>
> — ESTHER 7:2

When a man is in love with a woman, there is nothing he won't do for her. Esther was the queen of the kingdom and queen of his heart. He was willing to give half of all he had to her. This is what real love, respect, and honor are to your husband. You are his queen of everything.

Esther was a woman of excellence. Her response is astonishing.

> Then Queen Esther answered, 'If I have found favor with

you, Your Majesty, and if it pleases you, Your Majesty,
spare my life. That is my request. And spare the life of
my people. That is what I ask for.

— ESTHER 7:3

Notice her humble attitude, *"If I have found favor with you, Your
Majesty?"* As his wife, she didn't take for granted the favor and the
love he had for her. She addresses him as "Your Majesty." She was
his queen and did not have to call him, "Your Majesty." However,
he had just called her "Queen Esther" showing her respect and
honor. She was mirroring the love the two of them shared, recognizing his authority and his protection.

She goes on to say, *"If I have found favor with you, grant my life,
Your Majesty. This is my petition. Spare my people. This is my
request."*

And she continues...

You see, we—my people and I—have been sold so that we
can be wiped out, killed, and destroyed. If our men and
women had only been sold as slaves, I would have kept
silent because the enemy is not worth troubling you
about, Your Majesty.'"

— ESTHER 7:4

Esther knew what was and what was not important to her
husband. She understood her role as the Queen, and she understood when she needed his protection and authority.

I am the queen of questions. So, I asked myself, "Why couldn't Queen Esther tell the King at the first banquet?" The answer is simple for me. It wasn't the right time.

God was not finished changing the heart of the King. Just the way humans prepare for parties and events, God prepares in the same manner.

Between the first and second banquet, something significant and life-altering happened. King Artaxerxes needed to be reminded that Mordecai the Jew saved his life from a murderous plot. Now King Artaxerxes needed to acknowledge and bless the very Jew whose life was about to be taken along with the other Jews in the kingdom and the wife he loved.

An evil plot was about to be executed, and God would elevate and save every Jew in the kingdom. Esther was sensitive to the leading of God because God held her back from making the request at the first banquet.

There are times when God will show a wife something, but she needs to hold back until God gives her the okay to speak her mind. Esther didn't even have to hold the banquets. The King already told her he would give her up to half the kingdom, so why didn't she ask him then? Because the timing was off.

Ladies, learn your husband's behavior and be aware of the clues so that decisions can be made with wisdom and in a way that will bless you as a couple.

> Esther spoke again to the king. She fell down at his feet
>   crying and begged him to have mercy and to undo the
>   evil plot of Haman, who was from Agag, and his
>   conspiracy against the Jews. The king held out his

golden scepter to Esther, and Esther got up and stood in front of the king. She said, "Your Majesty, if it pleases you, and if I have found favor with you, if you consider my cause to be reasonable and if I am pleasing to you, cancel the official orders concerning the plot of Haman (who was the son of Hammedatha and was from Agag). He signed the order to destroy the Jews in all your provinces, Your Majesty. I cannot bear to see my people suffer such evil. And I simply cannot bear to see the destruction of my relatives. King Xerxes said to Queen Esther and Mordecai the Jew, "I have given Haman's property to Esther, and Haman's dead body was hung on the pole because he tried to kill the Jews. You write what you think is best for the Jews in the king's name. Seal it also with the king's signet ring, because whatever is written in the king's name and sealed with the king's signet ring cannot be canceled.

— ESTHER 8: 3-8

This love story between King Artaxerxes and Queen Esther continues. A bond of intimacy, love, respect, and honor deepen.

We find Esther going a second time before the King. This time, Esther is showing her feelings of despair. The King extended his scepter to her, but this time she doesn't touch it as she did the first time.

It was not because she was disrespectful or rude. It was because something had deepened in their relationship. God honored her, and He gave her something more important than half of the kingdom, a husband who honored her, respected her, and protected her. What a difference between Vashti and Esther.

Esther understood honor, respect, humility, and her role. Vashti was disrespectful, rude, and had no concept of how her attitude of pride would diminish the King.

Queen Esther and King Artaxerxes are celebrated throughout the world today. What an incredible love story.

Discussion For Couples and Groups:

King Artaxerxes' Strengths	King Artaxerxes' Weaknesses
Wasn't Arrogant, consulted his advisors (Esther 1:13-14)	Conceited
	Proud
	Rude
	Selfish
	Unforgiving
	Made Decisions in the Heat of Emotion
	Controlling
	Impatient
	Angry

Queen Esther's Strengths	Queen Esther's Weaknesses
Courage	Fear
Good Reputation	
Teachable	
Humble	
Wise	
Honest	
Honorable	
Intelligent	
Beautiful	
Self-Sacrificing	

The world does not understand the importance of godly behaviors and attitudes. How you act in a marriage or in a relationship will determine its success. Esther possessed many wonderful and extraordinary qualities, and they started with her personal relationship with God Himself. Then, by the advice of her godly uncle Mordecai, and then by the King's appointed eunuch Hegai.

Wisdom is found in the counsel of the godly. The Bible leads the path of the righteous. Even if Hegai the eunuch was not a godly man, he knew what was best and made sure Esther was chosen. God will use whomever He wants to make His will and plan come to fruition. Our job is to listen to advice and wisdom that makes sense, as Esther did successfully.

As a wife, Esther knew what her husband enjoyed, and she took all that into consideration when planning the banquet. There was no need for her to manipulate or deceive. With the perfect timing of the second banquet, King Artaxerxes was reminded of everything he had. He saw the admiration Esther had for him because of the effort she took to please him with the banquets. By doing so, she gave him the greatest gift she possessed by showing him all he had acquired and all of his success. To top it all off, she was doting on him.

The job of a wife and a queen, as when playing chess, is to protect her king. When you're protecting the king, you protect your kingdom, your home, and your future. Had she not stepped in to plead for her life and the lives of her people, bloodshed would have happened. God would have protected the seed of the Jewish people. But maybe not before a lot of them would have been put to death.

Notice the loyalty of Esther and the extent to which she went to protect him. That's called a loyal and faithful wife. What kind of man would not want this kind of woman? She sacrificed herself on behalf of the Jews and protected her husband from committing a horrific and evil act.

A wise, respectful, kind, loving, loyal, honorable, courageous, and teachable wife is a crown on the head of her husband. Men, when you are looking for a wife, as I tell my son, look for these attributes. And as I teach my daughter, I remind her that a woman of excellence possesses these qualities.

Esther was a beautiful woman. I often hear women say that it doesn't matter what they look like; the only thing that matters is the heart. Although beauty indeed comes from the heart, it is more than that. Esther was already beautiful when she was taken into the citadel. And yet, she was given beauty treatments for a year before she saw the King.

We live in a world where television and magazines are constantly bombarding us with the so-called perfect body. So many women are suffering from wrong ideas about their body image.

There is a happy medium. Taking care of your body is important because we are the temple of the Holy Spirit. Eating clean and grooming yourself to look presentable and lovely is not a sin. Sometimes I feel there is a lot of laziness within the Christian community to excuse bad behaviors.

God created everybody beautifully. There are no ugly people out there. What makes a person ugly is their attitude, self-hate, and the making of poor choices. It is important to take care of yourself, so you are presentable to your husband or wife. When you view yourself as ugly, you begin to make poor choices. But if you see yourself as God's greatest creation and view yourself as God's masterpiece, then you will make good choices that will honor Him.

Esther is an exceptional woman in grace, elegance, and wisdom. As I studied her life, I could only find one possible weakness: She was fearful of approaching the King. In keeping with honesty, I cannot fault her for that. Who could? Her life was in danger. But in the end, she conquered her fear. This is one of those cases where her greatest weakness became her greatest strength. Studying her inspires me, as it should you, to be this kind of a woman.

King Artaxerxes shows that he is conceited, controlling, rude, impatient, proud, selfish, unforgiving, and angry. As I read and studied this book, I realized two things that are very important for us to address and think about.

We find most of these weaknesses happening under one incident; the refusal of Vashti to appear before him and his guests. Before anyone tries to defend Vashti, we need to understand the custom in their day. She was the queen, and there were duties she needed to perform according to the Persian culture. While King Artaxerxes and his leaders partied, Vashti was partying with the wives of the leaders. Whatever took place at that moment in time when she refused to appear before the king, it was 100% her fault.

The only way to explain this is to look at any royal family today in our world. We know that royal families have a code of conduct and expectations that you and I would never agree with or receive.

What Vashti did was an act of defiance toward the King and the regulations set forth for her to carry out. Even if King Artaxerxes had these weaknesses brought on and instigated by Vashti deciding to go against her husband, the embarrassment she caused him was enormous.

The Persian Empire spread throughout three continents, almost half the world as we know it. Imagine that behavior spreading like wildfire, causing every leader to regret attending that party. King Artaxerxes was hurt and humiliated by the one he loved.

How do we know he loved her? Because he regretted putting her away, which caused him deep depression. If he was a womanizer, he wouldn't have cared that he put her away. He could have enjoyed any woman he wanted.

Regarding his burning anger, we find that mentioned twice: When Vashti refused to appear and when he heard Haman wanted to kill the queen. Again, those would be good reasons and appropriate responses to the wrong that took place.

We could say that his inability to forgive Vashti and his decision to banish her was poor judgment. However, I would argue that Vashti's attitude was deplorable while Esther's attitude was one of excellence. King Artaxerxes went down in history as a powerful man. Esther's influence made a difference in his success and blessings.

The King is intriguing. Let me explain. He was painted as this horrible, conceited man who only thought about himself. Then, when Esther broke the rules and appeared before him without being summoned, we found him kind, compassionate, loving, attentive, accommodating, and understanding.

How could he act one way with one wife and act a different way with another wife? Let me tell you why. He knew Esther truly loved him and wanted to please him. It's all about respect.

The most important thing to a man is his wife's honor and respect towards him. No matter how we look at it, the man is always the king of his home. A man knows when a woman truly honors, respects him and works toward building him up. This is one area that a wife cannot fake. Interestingly, this man would tell Esther that he would give her up to half of his kingdom without even knowing what the issue was. Either he was foolish and insane or a man completely in love who trusted his wife's judgment. I believe the latter.

King Artaxerxes honored his wife, Esther, by giving his signet ring to her Uncle Mordecai, whom he made second in command. The signet ring was the King's seal, used to seal legal documents. Once sealed with the signet ring, the law could not be revoked.

Only the king could decide who could use and hold that ring. In this case, Mordecai was favored by the King, and the King gave Mordecai his ring. What an honor! A godly wife brings honor not only to her husband but also to her family.

King Artaxerxes went to Esther and asked, *"What more would you like? Is there anything else I can do for you?"* She said, *"Yes. I want my people to be able to defend themselves against all those who are trying to kill them."* For two days, the Jews were allowed to defend themselves and kill all those who tried to kill them. After all of this, the King continues to honor his wife by declaring a holiday called Purim that is still observed and celebrated.

What can we learn from this amazing love story? God can use a godly woman to influence her husband to do great things, and she will bring him honor and blessings. Most importantly, there is a second chance for those who have been mistreated and abused by a previous spouse. King Artaxerxes and Queen Esther bring us hope.

CHAPTER 6

BOAZ & RUTH

The story of Ruth and Boaz shows that when you do things God's way, God supernaturally blesses you beyond imagination. Let's take a closer look at this beautiful love story.

Ruth was married to one of Naomi's sons, who was not a godly man. To understand Ruth, you have to know where she came from and who her people were. The Moabites were Israel's enemies, so you can understand why Ruth's husband was an ungodly man. God had strictly commanded the Israelites not to take pagan women or pagan men to be their spouses.

> Never marry any of them. Never let your daughters marry
> their sons or your sons marry their daughters.
>
> — DEUTERONOMY 7:3

Naomi's sons were in direct violation and opposition to God's laws. The God of Israel was not the god of the Moabites, and, knowing this, both of Naomi's sons married Moabite women.

Then, Naomi's husband and her two sons die, leaving her and her daughters-in-law alone. Can you see the disastrous consequences of going against the Word of God? However, in His mercy, compassion, and love, God rescues Naomi and Ruth because it's all about the heart.

> But Ruth answered, 'Don't force me to leave you. Don't make me turn back from following you. Wherever you go, I will go, and wherever you stay, I will stay. Your people will be my people, and your God will be my God. Wherever you die, I will die, and I will be buried there with you. May the Lord strike me down if anything but death separates you and me!'
>
> — RUTH 1:16-17

Talk about determination, boldness, and conviction. Naomi's mouth spoke out of the abundance of her heart. She followed through by acting on what she said. Her heart was faithful, moldable, and pliable. She left all she knew—her country, culture, family—and headed into an unknown land, knowing she would never be accepted.

Ruth showcased courage, strength, and flexibility in assimilating into a completely different country and culture, a new world to her. Ruth's new world became a blessing to Naomi and generations to come. Out of her lineage, King David was born, all the way to the Son of God, our Lord and Savior Jesus Christ. Do you see what happens when you have a heart that is moldable and pliable?

Naomi had a relative. He was from Elimelech's side of the

family. He was a man of outstanding character named Boaz. Ruth, who was from Moab, said to Naomi, 'Please let me go to the field of anyone who will be kind to me. There I will gather the grain left behind by the reapers.' Naomi told her, 'Go, my daughter.' So Ruth went. She entered a field and gathered the grain left behind by the reapers. Now it happened that she ended up in the part of the field that belonged to Boaz, who was from Elimelech's family. Just then, Boaz was coming from Bethlehem, and he said to his reapers, 'May the Lord be with all of you!' They answered him, 'May the Lord bless you!' Boaz asked the young man in charge of his reapers, 'Who is this young woman?' The young man answered, 'She's a young Moabite woman who came back with Naomi from the country of Moab. She said, 'Please let me gather grain. I will only gather among the bundles behind the reapers. So she came here and has been on her feet from daybreak until now. She just sat down this minute in the shelter.'

— RUTH 2:1-7

What's impressive is that Ruth did not wait to be cared for. Instead, she got up and worked in the field, gathering grain and maintaining her home. Ruth showed her independence and took responsibility for her life and Naomi's life.

Ruth did what was expected of her by gathering grain because she said, *"There I will gather the grain left behind by the reapers."*

God's commands dictated that one should leave a bundle of grain behind so the poor could gather it.

> When you are harvesting your crops and forget to bring in
> a bundle of grain from your field, don't go back to get it.
> Leave it for the foreigners, orphans, and widows. Then
> the LORD your God will bless you in all you do.
>
> — DEUTERONOMY 24:19

Somewhere, in this new world, Ruth learned the culture and the commands the Israelites lived by. She adapted to her surroundings and a new way of life.

> Naomi had a relative. He was from Elimelech's side of the
> family. He was a man of outstanding character named
> Boaz.
>
> — RUTH 2:1

God was leading her straight to the field of Boaz. Ruth worked hard all day. And then Boaz enters. Do you know what strikes me about this verse? Boaz picked her out.

Can you imagine this very wealthy, respectable, and prominent man noticing a young, poor, Moabite widow? After working in the field, I'm sure Ruth was perspiring from the hot sun, looking completely exhausted. And then to top everything off, with her hair a mess and dirt all over her, she wasn't wearing the best of clothes. So, ask yourself, what did Boaz see in Ruth that grabbed his attention? I suggest that there is an instant connection when God is leading you to His very best.

Next, we read that Boaz goes to her and addresses her as his daughter.

Boaz said to Ruth, 'Listen, my daughter. Don't go in any
other field to gather grain, and don't even leave this
one. Stay here with my young women. Watch where my
men are reaping, and follow the young women in that
field. I have ordered my young men not to touch you.
When you're thirsty, go to the jars and drink some of
the water that the young men have drawn.'

— RUTH 2:8-9

Here you see a picture of a man who truly loved a woman. Boaz, in
one simple, swift move, accomplished everything desired by any
woman on earth. He addressed her with honor and respect. He
told her not to go to any other field because she is welcome in his
field. He provided not just the protection of the women who work
with her but also warned the men not to lay hands on Ruth. Then,
he invited her to get a drink from the water jars the men had filled,
showing her she was not a beggar but a worker.

Boaz ministered to Ruth mentally, emotionally, spiritually, and
physically. That is what needs to happen in every relationship.
Let's take note of some very important points. The first point is
Ruth replied immediately by bowing down and thanking him. A
good woman recognizes what a great man has done for her.

'Why are you so helpful? Why are you paying attention to
me? I'm only a foreigner.'

— RUTH 2:10

There are two things she needed to know. First, she needed to
understand why he was so helpful and why he was paying her

attention. Secondly, she acknowledged his honoring, protecting, and providing for her. It was evident in her mind that Boaz was favoring her. But she needed to know why.

Men, pay close attention. When seeking a woman of character, integrity, and honor, you must be a man of character, integrity, and honor too. Don't expect to find the woman of your dreams if you are not paying attention. In addition, a woman of integrity, honor, and character will not give you the time of day if you do not demonstrate your love backed by actions. In other words, saying you love her is not enough. You either show the love you have for her, or you don't.

Ladies, hear me loud and clear as well; the Word of God is clear. We are to honor and respect our husbands, and we are expected to let them lead. Therefore, when you find a man who demonstrates these godly traits, do not disrespect him by dishonoring him or his wishes. I know I just dropped a bombshell, but I cannot go against what the Word of God says.

Obviously, we do not follow a man's lead that causes us to break the law of the land or the Law of God written in the Bible. However, you must show the respect, and honor Ruth showed to Boaz, her potential husband. Men want to be recognized, appreciated, and respected for the way they care for their woman (wife). In no way am I suggesting you bow down to the ground before him. What I am saying is that you show respect and honor in your actions. You see, Boaz told her what to do and how to do it. She neither argued nor disregarded what he told her.

Woman, recognize when a man is honoring you, protecting you, and providing for you by honoring him in ways that matter to him. Protect him against things that disparage him, degrade him, or insult him. Honor him before relatives and friends and do not allow them to come between the two of you in any way, shape, fashion, or form.

Finally, provide for him everything he needs spiritually, emotionally, mentally, and physically. Yes, Ladies, this means sex. Never withhold sex from your husband because you're angry.

Ladies, listen carefully to what Ruth says next: *"Why are you so helpful? Why are you paying attention to me? I'm only a foreigner."*

Do you see what she just did?

First, she paid her respects in an honorable manner. Then she boldly asked him, "Why her?" In other words, she knew he picked her, a foreigner, out of a whole crowd, blessing her such that he had her dip her bread in his bowl. He was already showing signs of love and attraction to her.

I love this because she was out, working, doing her thing, and the man of her dreams was watching and inquiring about her. Ruth was simply living her life and doing what she had to do. That's when Boaz came along. He had already been well-informed about Ruth and knew she was not an ordinary woman. Ladies, go about doing what you need to do with excellence, respecting yourself, others, and honoring God. The right man will find you too.

What happens next is unusual and a bit strange for our culture. However, in Deuteronomy 25:5-10, the laws and regulations dictated what must be done to marry a widow with no children. Boaz knew about this law and did accordingly. So now, Naomi instructs Ruth on what she must do.

> Naomi, Ruth's mother-in-law, said to her, 'My daughter, shouldn't I try to look for a home that would be good for you? Isn't Boaz, whose young women you've been

working with, our relative? He will be separating the barley from its husks on the threshing floor tonight. Freshen up, put on some perfume, dress up, and go down to the threshing floor. Don't let him know that you're there until he's finished eating and drinking. When he lies down, notice the place where he is lying. Then uncover his feet, and lie down there. He will make it clear what you must do.' Ruth answered her, 'I will do whatever you say.'

— RUTH 3:1-5

Ladies, Ruth had a heart for listening and obeying the instructions of the older woman. She did as she was told, even though it was not what she was accustomed to. There is wisdom and blessing when we choose to obey those whose lives are clearly demonstrating godly character.

Within the Christian community, we sometimes mistakenly assume the only thing a man is requiring when looking for a wife is her godly traits. Let me tell you that is false. A man looks at her appearance as well. Women make a grave mistake in thinking they don't have to dress up and take care of themselves.

Men, just as you are looking at the way a woman takes care of her appearance, she is looking at your appearance as well.

I ask, is there any woman on planet Earth who does not want to hear, *"I will do whatever you say,"* from the man she loves? Do you know why he so easily and freely made such a statement?

People have told me about everything you have done for your mother-in-law after your husband died. They told

me how you left your father and mother and the
country where you were born. They also told me how
you came to people that you didn't know before. May
the Lord reward you for what you have done! May you
receive a rich reward from the Lord God of Israel,
under whose protection you have come for shelter.

— RUTH 2:11-12

So, this is why it was so easy for Boaz to say to Ruth, *"I will do whatever you say."*

Ladies, your godly character and reputation will attract the eyes of a godly man. What you do and what you say will be told in his ears. You don't have to brag about a thing. Your reputation does your bragging for you.

When Boaz met Ruth, she bowed before him out of reverence and respect. Now he's bowing before her by uttering the words, *"I will do whatever you say."* If you don't catch anything else in this story, catch this: When you honor, respect, and protect your man, there isn't anything he won't do for you.

Men, it doesn't matter how old you are, if you wait on God's timing for the woman of your dreams, God will bring you a woman who will respect, honor, and protect you. This has been beautifully displayed by Ruth.

Ladies, a godly man who truly loves you will have a plan of action.

Boaz had a plan, and the plan was well thought out according to God's law and the laws of the land. His plan was genius.

Boaz went to the city gate and sat there. Just then, the rela-

tive about whom he had spoken was passing by. Boaz
said, "Please come over here and sit, my friend." So the
man came over and sat down.

Then Boaz chose ten men who were leaders of that city
and said, "Sit here." So they also sat down.

— RUTH 4:1-2

Boaz went to the place of business negotiations and called over the
man by addressing him as "friend." Right there, you see a man of
integrity, honor, and great character.

So, Boaz not only addressed this man as friend, he also invited the
man to sit down with him and the other ten fellow countrymen.
This showed respect and honor towards his fellow countryman
and also showed the regard Boaz had for Ruth and the Law
of God.

In doing this, he was protecting Ruth, providing for Ruth, and
protecting her reputation. That, Ladies, is a real man. But wait,
there's more. Let's dig deeper, shall we?

Boaz sets up the man in an intelligent and noble manner. For the
man to purchase the property, he would also have to take Ruth as
his wife. There was no other besides Boaz left to take Ruth.

'Boaz said to the man, 'Naomi, who has come back from
the country of Moab, is selling the field that belonged
to our relative Elimelech. So I said that I would inform
you. Buy it in the presence of these men sitting here
and in the presence of the leaders of our people. If you
wish to buy back the property, you can buy back the
property. But if you do not wish to buy back the prop-

erty, tell me. Then I will know that I am next in line because there is no other relative except me.' The man said, 'I'll buy back the property.' Boaz continued, 'When you buy the field from Naomi, you will also assume responsibility for the Moabite Ruth, the dead man's widow. This keeps the inheritance in the dead man's name.' The man replied, 'In that case I cannot assume responsibility for her. If I did, I would ruin my inheritance. Take all my rights to buy back the property for yourself, because I cannot assume that responsibility.'

— RUTH 4:3-6

He didn't come through the back door or through some hole in the wall. He came through the front door, doing it the right way with honor, respectability, and class.

Men, if you want a woman to bring you honor at the city gates, you must exercise your God-given right as a man to do things the honorable and respectable way. This distinguishes the man from the boy. May I remind every woman reading this to wait for the man and not waste time with the boy.

Boaz was older, he was discerning, wise, and judicious. He showed deep love and respect for Ruth. Ruth showed respect and honor for him by trusting him to bring out the desire of her heart. Her desire was to marry and have a family with Boaz.

At the end of this story, Boaz wins Ruth. Ruth receives the desires of her heart. This is a real love story about two people who did things God's way. How significant is this? Boaz and Ruth had a son named Obed. Obed had a son named Jesse, and then Jesse had a son named King David. But that's not all! Jesus Christ, our Lord, Savior, and Redeemer, came through this lineage.

Do you understand this yet? First, God redeemed, restored, and rescued Ruth. And then God esteemed, elevated, and exalted Boaz.

Ladies and Gentlemen, there isn't anyone that I know of on Planet Earth who does not want a marriage like this.

At the very beginning of this story, Ruth made this statement, *"Your God shall be my God."* Here is where everything begins and ends. What matters most to God is a heart that fervently, steadfastly, and faithfully seeks after Him and His ways. If you are looking to have the blessings of God fall on you and want the blessings of God to fall on your marriage, then you must do things God's way!

Discussion For Couples and Groups:

Ruth's Strengths	Ruth's Weaknesses
Kind (Ruth 1:16-18)	Boaz
Compassionate (Ruth 2:18)	
Loving (Ruth 1:14-18)	
Respectful (Ruth 2:2)	
Responsible (Ruth 2:17-18)	
Honorable (Ruth 3:6)	
Noble (Ruth 2:11-12)	
Of Good Reputation (Ruth 2:11-12)	

Boaz's Strengths	Boaz's Weaknesses
Kind (Ruth 2:8-12)	Ruth
Compassionate (Ruth 2:14-16)	
Loving (Ruth 3:10-13)	
Respectful (Ruth 4:1-3)	
Responsible (Ruth 4:5-10)	
Protective (Ruth 2:15-16)	
Honorable (Ruth 4:13-17)	
Good Provider (Ruth 2:14)	
Of Good Reputation (Ruth 4:14-15)	
Godly (Ruth 4:1-10)	
Patient (Ruth 3:10)	
Wise (Ruth 4:1-10)	
Understanding (Ruth 3:11-13)	

The world doesn't understand that to receive the blessings of God, one must relinquish their will and their ways (all that they know) to bring about blessings in every aspect of their lives. If you want to see God's blessings in your home, then you have to choose to reject what displeases God and reject seeking human approval.

The only weakness of Ruth and Boaz is that they were love-struck over each other. Obviously, it's a great weakness to have.

I mention this because of the two statements which have been made by them both. From the moment Boaz spoke to Ruth, his heart exploded with love for her. Could it be that Boaz exuded so much love for her through his words and actions that not even Boaz himself realized how much he demonstrated his love for her? And could it be that he demonstrated so much love that his own workers noticed how he fell instantly in love with her? Telling the young men who worked for him not to lay a hand on her spoke volumes. His statement, *"I will do whatever you say,"* is a continuation of the deep love, respect, and honor he had for her. Please understand this was not a weakness by any means. But rather an important strength every man should have for his wife.

Ruth's weakness was that she was respectably bold in doing two things. Upon meeting, the first thing she asked was, *"Why are you so helpful? Why are you paying attention to me?"* and the second thing was when she went into his tent and laid down at his feet. By laying down at his feet, she was basically asking him what his intentions were, that she was ready and wanted to be his wife.

Ladies, it's perfectly okay to set the record straight at the beginning of a relationship.

We do things God's way, not the world's way. In a marriage covenant, you certainly should be bold to express your feelings, concerns, and aspirations with your husband in a respectful and uplifting manner.

CHAPTER 7

THE SHULAMITE WOMAN & KING SOLOMON

The love story between the Shulamite Woman and Solomon is extraordinary. It beautifully showcases the burning desire and pure love between two lovers. We are the awkward spectators as we read the passionate exchange of words and actions of intimacy between husband and wife.

Sex is a gift from God to a married couple to enjoy exclusively with each other. It is to be kept between husband and wife because sex without the commitment of marriage is cheap and meaningless. God did not create sex to be used frivolously or casually. He created sex as a beautiful experience, filled with emotions and eroticism between a husband and wife.

Sex is sacred, and the marriage bed needs to be kept pure, holy, and within the confines of how God created sex to be. Sex is NOT unclean, filthy, or grubby. It is, however, pleasurable, blissful, and creates a bond between husband and wife that is indescribable. Therefore, in a godly manner, we will discuss the beauty and importance of the sexual act between a husband and wife.

Let's look closely at this intensely passionate couple, Solomon and The Shulamite.

> Wear me as a signet ring on your heart, as a ring on your hand. Love is as overpowering as death. Devotion is as unyielding as the grave. Love's flames are flames of fire, flames that come from the Lord. Raging water cannot extinguish love, and rivers will never wash it away.
>
> — SONG OF SOLOMON 8:6-7

This is what real love looks like, Folks.

True love is an act of will, and it is a commitment. Lust, however, demands immediate satisfaction while requiring no commitment. Love always begins in the heart. It's a strong and passionate emotion. You can actually feel the love you have for someone.

Let me explain how a signet ring works and its relevance to marriage. The signet ring is an original identifying symbol of the king. The law the King put into effect was irrevocable. So, he would take his signet ring, dip it in hot wax, then seal the document with the imprint from his ring. Do you see how beautiful and powerful this is? The Shulamite's desire and love for her husband was uncontrollable, fervent, and intense. She wanted to be permanently sealed upon his heart.

The Shulamite declared what it is like to try to quench love.

> Wear me as a signet ring on your heart,
> as a ring on your hand.
> Love is as overpowering as death.
> Devotion is as unyielding as the grave.

Love's flames are flames of fire,
flames that come from the Lord. Raging water cannot
    extinguish love,
and rivers will never wash it away.
If a man exchanged all his family's wealth for love,
people would utterly despise him.

— SONG OF SOLOMON 8:6-7

In other words, their love burned like fire for each other, and nothing was able to stop that.

Love begins in the heart as emotion and grows into commitment.

Song of Solomon 8:6-7 is often used in wedding ceremonies and on wedding invitations because it speaks to the commitment of love and marriage. The seal, then, continues by committing to each other in the marriage ceremony and the exchanging of vows.

The Shulamite was obvious in her passion and desire for Solomon and what she wanted from him. She wanted him to keep her in his heart, holding her as dearly as she did him.

Their love spiraled into the physical act of lovemaking. Please catch this: This applies to both males and females, especially to women. Be bold and stand your ground. When it comes to real love, you deserve all three, the emotion, the commitment, and the physical. Ladies, don't buy into the lie that having sex with a man, outside of marriage, will guarantee a seal upon his heart, or on your finger. Genuine emotional love always leads to protection, honor, and integrity. Those things can only take place with commitment.

Ladies, a true man of God protects you by understanding that purity before God matters. Therefore, he will be concerned about what God thinks of your relationship. In addition, he will be concerned about his relationship with God. All of this, in combination, will bring about a pure relationship that pleases God, resulting in marriage.

A godly husband will praise you for saving yourself for him as Solomon praised the Shulamite's virginity.

> My bride, my sister is a garden that is locked, a garden that
>   is locked, a spring that is sealed.

> — SOLOMON 4:12

Let me explain what this means. In the Jewish Tradition, it means the Shulamite had kept her innocence and purity, and she was now able to give that to her husband as a gift.

> That's why a man will leave his father and mother and be
>   united with his wife, and the two will be one.

> — EPHESIANS 5:31

Sex is sacred and, therefore, deserves to be reserved for marriage.

What happens if you are divorced, had a past before Christ, or are a Christian who has fallen and repented? The good news is that once you repent, God has thrown your sin into the Sea of Forgetfulness. He has restored you, giving you a clean slate. As difficult as it is for those who are divorced, you need to keep yourself pure until God sends you someone to love for a lifetime. Those with past sexual immorality, before Christ, are now a new creature in

Christ, your old life is gone. Therefore, you can walk in purity before God as you wait on Him to send you your love for a lifetime.

Note the importance of praising each other and really meaning what you say. From chapter to chapter, you see the Shulamite Woman and Solomon praising each other. They are very graphic in what they say to each other, both in and out of lovemaking. In marriage, sex does NOT start in the bedroom. It is how you behave and love each other throughout the day to create an atmosphere of romance.

There is absolutely nothing wrong with anything the Shulamite and Solomon said to each other. It is normal, expected, and required to sustain a marriage. In other words, it is perfectly normal to lust after your own spouse and think about how your day is going to end. God created sex as the ultimate and most pleasurable expression of love you and your spouse can enjoy. Sex is the ultimate ecstasy. Therefore, it should be treasured.

There's an important verse we need to look at:

> Young women of Jerusalem, swear to me that you will not awaken love or arouse love before its proper time!
>
> — SONG OF SONGS 8:4

This statement, made by the Shulamite, was so important that she repeated it three times. When you have a verse repeated more than once in a book, one needs to pay close attention, especially since Song of Songs only has eight chapters.

Our society has made love unrecognizable. Loving yourself and loving your body does not involve giving it away freely to multiple sex partners. Somehow society has portrayed love as cheap and tawdry. However, that's not the idea of love. The Shulamite Woman was simply saying wait before you emotionally connect, commit, and get physical. Again, love is an emotion that is felt. And once love is felt, you want to express that love with action. But this cannot happen without commitment. This is what the Shulamite was saying. As young as she was, she understood the wisdom in warning the young women of Jerusalem not to awaken love with just anyone. In other words, you too will get to experience this ecstasy, but it must be in the confines of marriage.

The Shulamite Woman and Solomon had a deep connection and love for each other. They were lovers, confidants, and best friends. If I ever believed in a soulmate, this would be the best example. They appreciated one another, and they respected one another. Their language of love had no boundaries and no limits. Their hearts were opened to each other. They were each other's equal. He elevated her with words of admiration and honored her values which led to great respect, causing pride to swell up in his heart. They belonged to each other, and they both knew it. Their love was spontaneous and affectionately displayed differently, as we can see throughout this book. That should speak loudly. We do not withhold our bodies from the one we are married to. It is also essential to note the freedom between the two lovers as their marriage progresses and develops, thus allowing them to enjoy conversational and physical intimacy. It is a privilege and an honor when someone finds a mate to have this kind of relationship with.

I know this kind of passion exists. I can understand why the Shulamite spoke so strongly to the women of Jerusalem.

Today, we can learn much from her example of purity and wisdom. The Shulamite clearly understood the need to be emotionally ready. Emotional readiness means you are equally prepared for a commitment. Therefore, when you are emotionally ready, you are passionate, ardent, and intense. There is an awareness and understanding of the next step in commitment. Commitment is an obligation you are willing to take on and be responsible for. Commitment involves pledging yourself to the one you want to be with for a lifetime, including bringing your relationship with the one you are committed to before God and witnesses in the marriage ceremony. You are attached to the person you are committed to, meaning you are stuck like glue to that person. Your allegiance is to that person alone, meaning you will be faithful until death do you part. No spareribs on the side. You are attached to the one you are committed to, meaning that person is by your side as the old cliché says, "Attached at the Hip." You are constant with the one you commit to, meaning you are stable, steadfast, and resolute in all your actions, thus proving your commitment to the one you love. When you commit yourself, you take on obligation, responsibility, loyalty, and reliability to the one you chose as your love for a lifetime.

Once you are emotionally ready and the commitment is made, then the fullness of that loving commitment is expressed in the act of lovemaking. That is your final piece that completes your relationship.

So, let's explain the physical in plain and simple English: Sex. You are concerned with your partner's sexual needs and desires. The chemistry between you and your spouse is expressed liberally and freely in the confines of your marriage.

When it comes to your spouse's body belonging to you and your body belonging to your spouse, consideration for your spouse plays a major role in the act of sex. Hear me clearly. There are things you should never allow into the bedroom. The world's view of sex does not hold the same value, respect, and honor. For instance, the Bible speaks against sodomy. He created sex for pleasure between husband and wife. Since He is the Creator of the gift of sex, He put rules in place for our protection. Man wants to defy what is good and perfect and take up what is evil and self-serving. Women, never allow yourselves to be used by men in sick, twisted, and sadistic sexual practices.

Lovemaking is a beautiful expression between two people who are deeply in love, committed to each other, and expressing it in the most intimate way that brings the ultimate ecstasy. Lovemaking starts in the morning when you wake up and continues with your expressions of love throughout the day until the day ends. Some examples of expressions of love throughout the day include sending a text message to your spouse, leaving a written note where you know your spouse will find it, or a quick phone call to say I love you. These things fan the fire of your marriage and keep it alive. Your spouse will have no reason to become emotionally connected to anyone else but you. You are keeping them committed to you. Then, you get to express it when you come together. This is what the young woman was talking about. Wow! How wise was the Shulamite Woman!

We come to my favorite Bible verse:

> Who is this young woman coming from the wilderness
> with her arm around her beloved?

> — SONG OF SOLOMON 8:5

This Bible verse is rich in meaning. The maidens call out with delight, amazement, wonder, and awe. *Who is this young woman?*

The young woman has kept herself pure. She exhibits self-respect, honor, and integrity. She is filled with wisdom, courage and clothed in strength. She knows what she wants and knows how to bring it about. She participates in building up her lover and is proud to be by his side. The Shulamite Woman was not afraid of hard work and was doing her daily routine when Solomon found her.

The love story between the Shulamite and Solomon is one of the greatest romances in history. It shows us what marriage should look like. Every woman wants to be a Cinderella looking for her Prince. Look no further. This is a real-life dream come true as the Shulamite goes from wearing rags to royal robes, from the vineyard to the palace. No wonder the women of Jerusalem couldn't believe who was coming out of the desert. Here was the Shulamite coming out of a place of desolation, a place of barrenness, a place she probably thought she'd never leave. However, she still kept her morals and her high standards. Finally, the day came when God lifted her out of the wasteland. The wasteland was a place of gloom, sorrow, and unhappiness. God came and placed her in the arms of her beloved. She was cherished, adored, and treasured. In other words, she was dearly beloved and dear to his heart. What an ending to an incredible love story. The women of Jerusalem couldn't stop commending, admiring, and extolling the Shulamite and her King. When you decide to do things God's way, God takes notice and brings you the finest and most excellent gifts.

It doesn't matter where you are in life, whether you are single, never been married, widowed, or divorced, God has the very best for you. He is writing your love story.

Just because you're not married right now doesn't mean your day will not come. The years you spend without a life partner are not wasted. It might feel like it is a desert. You might be wary of waiting for so long. God Himself is your spouse. He is the best friend you could ever ask for. He is truly your Savior, your Deliverer, your Protector, your Provider, and the Lover of your soul. He is right there in the midst of your wilderness. We are the Bride (the Church) of Christ. Therefore, when we speak of God being your spouse, we speak in biblical terms that explain who the Body of Believers are to God. When the right mate comes for you, God will take you out of the wilderness and place you in the arms of your Beloved. Do not awaken love with anyone who is not meant for you. Wait for the one who can be the kind of mate we have read about in Song of Songs.

Discussion For Couples and Groups:

The Shulamite's Strengths	The Shulamite's Weaknesses
Pure	Didn't take care of herself as she should have
Genuine	
High Morals and Standards	
Self-Respect	
Respect for Future Spouse	
Inquisitive	
Considerate	
Sure of Herself	
Expressive	
Attentive to Husband's Needs	
Wise	
Confident	
Self-Acceptance	
Innocent	

Solomon's Strengths	Solomon's Weaknesses
	Spiritually Impure
Genuine	Insincere (700 wives, 300 concubines)
Wisdom	Womanizer
Considerate	No Self-Respect
Sure of himself	No Respect for Future Spouse
Expressive	Lack of Consideration for Wives
Attentive to Her Needs	Selfish
Confident	Egotistical
Self-Acceptance	Disobedient to God

The world doesn't understand the sacredness of intimacy between a man and a woman. Unfortunately, this precious gift is frequently given away cheaply to anyone because of physical urges and desires. The problem with this loose immoral mentality is that it brings more emotional difficulties and attachments to those you become intimate with.

Intimacy with a man is more than a physical act for a woman. It's an emotional connection. When a woman is having sex, her emotions participate in the physical act. Women are all about feelings. This is why women have a difficult time getting over a relationship after it ends. It is excruciating and hard to go through.

For a man, sex is purely physical. It is an urge they want to satisfy, and it really doesn't matter if they have feelings for the woman or not. They can sleep with one woman one day and another the next day. A relationship where people give themselves away so freely without anything in return is cheap and meaningless. In return, almost all the time, there is regret on the part of the woman. She feels used, hurt, and heartbroken.

From the Song of Songs, we clearly see that God is the Giver of the most amazing gift He could give us. God is not a killjoy. As people, we forget that He created the gift of lovemaking, and He created it as the ultimate joy and pleasure. The key to experiencing this ultimate ecstasy is sharing this physical act with the one you love. The act of lovemaking will never be truly satisfying if there is no love between the spouses.

If sex were not meant to be enjoyed, and if sex were grubby or filthy, God would not have dedicated an entire book to the sexual intimacy between a man and woman. God is letting you know sex is beautiful, amazing, and the expression of human love at its highest level.

This is the reason why we set up boundaries, and we don't cross those boundaries until "love is awakened." When you fall in love with someone, you have awakened love in your heart. You are now emotionally ready to take it to the next level, commitment. You pledge your endless love to that person, and you take those vows before God and man. You nourish the love spiritually, emotionally, mentally, and then you bring it to the physical act of lovemaking. In other words, you can't start the physical and work your way back to the emotional. It is a huge mistake, and one you will greatly pay for mentally, if you start a physical relationship before you are ready emotionally and committed in marriage. Just because a guy is having sex with you, Ladies, doesn't mean he loves you or is committed to you. I cannot believe how many times I have heard a woman tell me, "But we had sex. I thought he loved me. He's a Christian." My response has always been, "If he was a 'Christian,' he would have acted like a godly man and done things the right way. He would not have compromised you. He would not have used you in an ugly and self-serving way."

Ladies, I've said this before, and I'm going to say it again: A man who truly loves you will make a connection with you emotionally and immediately bring it to the commitment level. The Commitment Level means he is pledging himself to you and only you, which translates to a marriage proposal. The Marriage Proposal will lead to the physical act of lovemaking. This is how you will know if the man who pursues you is truly in love with you. A godly man who has pure intentions will protect your honor and not disgrace you by placing you in a compromising situation. He will protect your integrity, watch over your character, and present you as the queen of his heart. Do not allow a boy to play the role of a man in your life.

Men, as a woman, I understand some women play the field. Their whole purpose is to party, have fun, and not be emotionally committed to anyone. Their whole point is to entice a man by getting him aroused. There is also the other type of woman who desperately wants to be married. She is the one who will have sex with a man hoping he will want to marry her by her giving him the physical act. The problem with this is that you can never put the physical act before the emotional act. It's not the act of sex that makes you fall in love with the person. You fall in love with the spirit of that person.

No man will commit to marriage because a woman has sex with him. The only way a commitment will take place is if a man loves her. The deep love he has for her will translate to commitment. This is why a man should not allow a woman to manipulate or deceive him.

Men, a woman who loves you will be concerned with your reputation. She wants the world to know that she married the man of her dreams. She wants everyone to know he is a godly man who leads their home and leads her by the way God wants him to. She does not want a weak man who is unfaithful, untrustworthy, and irresponsible. A woman who has sex with you, outside of marriage without an emotional connection and a commitment, is setting you up to bring you down. She will ruin your life with consequences that affect your future relationship with the possibility of losing the right woman. Let me be clear here: I'm talking about a possible unplanned pregnancy, the embarrassment of all who know you knowing what you did and blocking the blessings God has for you.

Men, here is your warning: Run away from these kinds of women. Wait for the godly one who will stand by your side, be your cheerleader and best friend, and who will love and support all your needs. Men, if you are already married to the love of your life, do everything you can to maintain your relationship with your wife.

By the way, I stand by the Word of God when we are commanded to not be unequally yoked. This means the one to whom you have committed yourself should be serving the same God as you. In other words, if you are a born-again Christian, you should not be marrying someone who is not a born-again Christian. If you got saved after you got married, you are obligated to continue being the godly influence in your spouse's life and to follow the commands of God.

Let's look at the strengths and weaknesses of the Shulamite and Solomon.

In this love story, we see a young woman of excellence. She is called the Shulamite. The Shulamite was genuine, pure, and innocent. Simply put, she was a virgin. Her husband glowed with pride and honor because of it. Solomon praised her for her virginity. That, Ladies and Gentlemen, is the key to a beautiful lovemaking experience. As we discussed in this book already, you can still present yourself before your husband if you come before him in the same manner, if you have repented of your past, or if you have been divorced or widowed. You can still remain untouched until God brings you your life partner.

The Shulamite had everything Solomon wanted for himself. On their honeymoon, she welcomed him to come to her and make love. She willingly opened herself to him, exposing her vulnerability to him as her husband.

The Shulamite had not just reserved herself for marriage but welcomed her husband *"to take from her garden its choice fruits."* No one had touched her before Solomon. She was a virtuous woman who possessed self-respect, high standards, and morals. Interestingly enough, this translates to great respect for her future husband. She guarded herself so that not just anyone could touch her but only the man she would marry and only on her wedding night.

We can learn from the Shulamite. She was unashamed and was not embarrassed when she presented herself to Solomon on their wedding night. She had not defiled herself. This is what she said to Solomon:

> Awake, north wind! Come, south wind! Blow on my
> garden! Let its spices flow from it. Let my beloved come
> to his garden, and let him eat his own precious fruit.
>
> — SONG OF SONGS 4:16

Wow! Very powerful! Who doesn't want this kind of a honeymoon? I think it's safe to say the Shulamite was quite sure of herself. She was quite creative in her expression of verbal intimacy to Solomon, such as...

> My beloved is a pouch of myrrh that lies at night between
> my breasts,

— SONG OF SONGS 1:13

Her greatest strength is understanding her husband's needs.

Ladies and Gentlemen, we all know we are made to be sexual creatures. However, to believe that sex is our only need would be unwise. Everything you are and all you do creates a marriage like Solomon and the Shulamite had. That means both spouses have to meet the other's emotional, mental, and physical needs. All of that works together along with open and transparent communication with each other.

The Shulamite's wisdom is admirable when she warned the women of Jerusalem not to awaken love until it was ready. She knew the importance of emotional commitment and physical commitment. She knew which came first and knew how to meet her husband's needs. She was adored, respected, and beloved by her husband in the process.

The Shulamite's weakness was that she didn't have time to care for herself before marriage because she worked out in the vineyards. However, it wasn't the outward appearance that attracted Solomon, but rather the pride and self-confidence she must have exhibited.

> Stop staring at me because I am so dark. The sun has
> tanned me. My brothers were angry with me. They

made me the caretaker of the vineyards. I have not even taken care of my own vineyard.

— SONG OF SOLOMON 1:6

Ladies, you must take care of yourself. I am not saying you have to look like you stepped off the runway of a fashion show. But I am saying you should make yourself presentable to your husband. And Men, that goes for you too.

Solomon was not shy or afraid to express his love verbally to his wife. Men and women must learn to express themselves emotionally to evoke and awaken a response from their spouses.

Lovemaking starts in the morning and finishes at night. Choose something that you love about your spouse in their appearance. For example, if your husband or wife has a beautiful smile, then comment on how his or her smile lights up your world and how you can't wait to see that smile again when you come home from work. We say the eyes are the window to the soul. So, if your wife or husband has an expression that makes you melt, you can express that to your spouse by saying, "I can't wait to see that look tonight." In saying something like this, you are pouring into each other's heart as Solomon did when he said to the Shulamite...

You are a spring for gardens, a well of living water flowing from Lebanon.

— SONG OF SOLOMON 4:15

It is essential to refresh your love for each other daily to maintain and grow your marriage. Your marriage is the most important thing after God. Therefore, it should be a priority first thing in the morning. Let me explain why.

By addressing your spouse first thing in the morning, you revitalize the love between the two of you. The same way you might grab a cup of coffee to wake yourself up, you are energizing your relationship through the way you communicate with each other. In other words, your lovemaking just started and will conclude at the end of the day.

Sex does not start in the bedroom. You stimulate your spouse throughout the day by sending a text message or a song that means something to the both of you. Or you give your spouse a quick phone call. You can even put a love note where you know they will find it, such as in the wallet or coat pocket on a bright piece of paper so it can't be missed. Couples must work very hard at their relationship as husband and wife.

At the end of the day, when you see each other again—unless someone is dead, dying, or bleeding—honor your word when you told your spouse that his or her smile lights up your world. By doing this straightforward exercise, you make your relationship deeper, bulletproof, and unbreakable. Do you see what you just did? You have been talking lovingly and sensually throughout the day, which has increased your level of communication and stimulated intimacy with your spouse, leaving you both feeling exhilarated after the day. Then, after all of this, you can handle whatever problems come your way together.

Solomon was genuine in his expression and attentive to the needs and desires of the Shulamite. In the process, his needs and desires were completely met by her. How do I know this? Because of Song of Songs Chapter 4. Even though in our English, his description of his bride doesn't entice us, it still has great meaning.

> Your hair is like a flock of goats moving down Mount
> Gilead.

> — SONG OF SONGS 4:1

To understand this correctly, we need to know what and where
Mount Gilead is. This mountain, also known as Mount Gilboa, is
1,696 feet above sea level. The lower slopes are very fertile. Vegeta-
tion is abundant, and the very best goats are found grazing there.
When you observe a healthy goat, you see the beauty and the love-
liness of their hair. So, what Solomon was saying was, "Your hair is
gorgeous, beautiful, and lovely," and, catch this, it also means
pleasing to the senses. Whatever she put in her hair, it enticed
him. He covered all the bases. He was saying to her that her hair
brought him pleasure. Now, don't you want to be told that your
hair looks like a flock of goats?

Solomon even went so far as complimenting her dental hygiene,
her smile, her teeth.

> Your teeth are like a flock of sheep about to be sheared,
> sheep that come up from the washing. All of them bear
> twins, and not one has lost its young.

> — SONG OF SONGS 4:2

The shepherds took good care of their sheep, which means they
took the sheep down to the body of water and washed them. In
other words, her teeth were symmetrically perfect, both upper and
lower teeth, with a smile that lit up his world. There were not any
missing or crooked teeth in her mouth. I must ask, who doesn't
want to be told that their teeth look like a flock of shorn sheep?

The Shulamite understood perfectly what he was saying because she would have known what the representation meant when he expressed himself using these comparative descriptions.

Here is one more example...

Your lips are like scarlet thread. Your mouth is lovely.

— SONG OF SONGS 4:3

Of all the things he said about her, I believe this is the most important. Please catch this truth: If you want a successful marriage, implement this very thing. Let the words out of your mouth be filled with hope, encouragement, love, and words that will restore and revive.

I find it interesting that Solomon used the phrase, "like scarlet thread." Do not put up walls of words between you and your spouse. I personally don't believe in fighting. Fighting is a terrible way to solve any issue. It's all about what comes out of your mouth and how you say it.

There's an important point here. Remember Rahab's scarlet thread hanging from the window? I believe this has great significance to what Solomon was saying. Rahab did not put her trust in the walls of the city she lived in; she trusted God for her deliverance. The Hebrew armies knew Rahab put the scarlet thread in the window so she would be delivered and not fall under the destruction the rest of the city would go through. She was the great-great-great-grandmother of Solomon (1 Chronicles 2:11-14). Rahab saved her family and herself because of the words she uttered (Joshua 2:8-12). Get my point now?

No wonder Solomon understood the power of words and wanted to kiss the Shulamite's lips.

You can see his strengths come alive as he demonstrates genuine love toward the Shulamite. He shows wisdom in using life-affirming words, and he is considerate of her needs and desires. He complimented her and was sure of himself in what he was saying. He was attentive to her needs as he communicated the language of love to his wife, which is what women desire and need. In turn, the Shulamite infused Solomon with life-affirming words. And because of those words, he was self-confident and had self-respect. Pride was swelling up in his heart, and he was over-whelmed with love. You could say he was a man who was deeply in love with his wife. It's all about your words.

Solomon's weaknesses cost him everything. He was the wisest man in the Bible. But for such a wise man, he made some terrible and tragic decisions. Under Jewish law, according to Deuteronomy 7:2-4, the Israelites were not to marry foreign wives, meaning they could not marry wives who were not serving the God of Israel because they would lead their hearts away from Him. This very act caused Solomon's downfall. He married women who turned his heart away from worshipping the God of Israel, leading him to worship false gods and commit idolatry. He made unwise deci-sions by marrying wives who served other gods and disobeyed God. Eventually, he had little regard for God's command. In doing this, he became insensitive to the needs of himself and that of his wife. He ended up with 700 wives and 300 concubines. He showed no respect for the wives or himself in marrying all these wives and having these concubines. He had no time to love them the way they needed to be loved. Solomon cheated himself out of the love he should have received. Now, do you understand why he kept marrying more and more women? Can you imagine that? How is that fair to him and the women he married? It would take him almost two years before he could see each wife once. No marriage can survive paying attention to your spouse once every two years.

Solomon's actions turned him into a womanizer, which made him inconsiderate of the women he married. That is no longer love but rather perverted unfilled sexual desires. No man or woman can be fulfilled physically, emotionally, and spiritually while engaging in sexual immorality. It only leaves one wanting more and more with no satisfaction. This is truly sad.

When you decide to disobey (for both men and women), you open yourself to all kinds of things. This means you are opening yourself to spiritual impurity. If you defy God, you are serving yourself. And in serving yourself, you dethrone God. Therefore, that makes you spiritually impure.

Solomon became conceited, vain, and egotistical. The opposite of egotistical is humility, self-sacrifice, and generosity. Get this: In marriage, you must possess these three traits, whether you are a man or a woman. Humility is forgiving your spouse, apologizing when needed, and appreciating your spouse. Self-sacrifice is laying down your wishes and looking out for the best interest of the one you love. In other words, you are becoming selfless.

Finally, in a marriage, generosity must abound. The more you give of yourself, the more you will receive. Those who are generous will find themselves blessed.

Solomon and the Shulamite's love story is one of my favorites. It clearly portrays a deep and meaningful love that incorporates the emotional, spiritual, and physical aspects. We see them coming together, creating an explosion. The Shulamite comes out from among the rest of the women from a dry and weary place, a desert.

She is paraded throughout the streets of Jerusalem on the arm of her beloved with cheers of praise, excitement, and acclamation. What a beautiful scene.

> Who is this young woman coming up from the wilderness
> like clouds of smoke? She is perfumed with myrrh and
> incense made from the merchants' scented powders.
> Look! Solomon's sedan chair... King Solomon had a
> carriage made for himself from the wood of Lebanon.
> He had its posts made out of silver, its top out of gold,
> its seat out of purple fabric. Its inside—with inlaid
> scenes of love—was made by the young women of
> Jerusalem. Young women of Zion, come out and look at
> King Solomon! Look at his crown, the crown his
> mother placed on him on his wedding day, his day of
> joyful delight.
>
> — SONG OF SONGS 3:6-7 & 9-11

Can you picture this scene with me? Can you see the excitement and joy of the newlyweds? I would like to be the Shulamite, wouldn't you, Ladies? And men, wouldn't you like to be wearing your crown? The desire of every mother is to prepare her son to be a good husband to his wife. A good wife, who is worth far more than rubies, is the glory and the crown of her husband.

This couple is an example and the epitome of what true, godly marriage should imitate. May I suggest, Men, that when you look for a wife, find one that meets these expectations and then some. And, Ladies, find a husband who will treat you like a real queen.

CHAPTER 8

THE LESSONS WE LEARN

The heart of God has always been for couples and for marriage. God understood it was not good for man to be alone from the very beginning of time. God saw it was not good for man to be alone when the world God had made was already perfect. We need to stop right there and understand this truth.

Imagine Adam was in a perfect place. His world was perfect. He didn't have to work the land. He didn't have to cook anything. He didn't have to wash or clean anything, and he had the companionship of every animal, tall and short, big and small. God saw Adam needed something other than the companionship of animals. Therefore, God created a helpmate for him. And out of Adam, Eve was created.

Consider the significance and reason Eve was created. I often ask myself the question, "Why couldn't God just ask Adam what he was looking for in a companion, how he wanted her to look and be, and why wasn't he allowed to watch God create her from the dust as he had him?" You see, God is all-wise and all-knowing. He knows what makes us tick. He knew what Adam would find attractive, and He knew exactly what Adam needed. Instead of creating Eve from the dust, He chose to put Adam to sleep (God's anesthesia process) and, instead, took a rib from his side to create Eve. We hear it all the time at marriage ceremonies, "Flesh of my flesh, bone of my bone."

God took one of the ribs from Adam's side to send a loud message to Adam and to those to come, "Your wife is to be by your side because she came from your side." She came from his flesh. Anything that hurts her should hurt you. She came from your bone, and anything that breaks in her should break in you because she came from your rib.

Ribs, medically speaking, are very fragile and very painful when broken. As a matter of fact, ribs play a huge role in our bodies. Every time you breathe, you feel the ribs being used. Every time you talk, the ribs are used. Every movement you make, so do your ribs. Ribs also protect the chest cavity. And ribs hold your body up because it is jointly connected to your spinal vertebrae. Many vital organs are protected by ribs, including the heart and the lungs. Can you see this picture now with much more clarity as to why God might have done what He did in creating Eve for Adam?

Ribs have a part to play in protecting your heart, and without your heart, you're dead. Your heart should beat for the person you love. It also protects the lungs. Remember when you first saw the one you fell in love with? He or she took your breath away. And finally, that rib plays an important role in keeping the spinal vertebrae intact. It is what keeps you up and standing, moving and walking. I could write an entire book on this.

The Bible gives a very interesting truth on the heart that we need to take seriously.

> Guard your heart more than anything else, because the
> source of your life flows from it.

> — PROVERBS 4:23

Clearly, the heart holds the emotions, and whatever is in the heart comes out of your mouth.

Men, your wife is the heart of the home. If she does not feel loved and if you don't take care of her, the heartbeat of your home will stop. Ladies, since you are the heart of the home, you are the one who keeps the flame burning. So, keep the flame burning in your husband by protecting, respecting, and honoring your husband. He is your protector, like the rib protects the heart in the body. In other words, this is what God did. He took the rib out of Adam, and He shaped and sculpted Eve to be the counterpart for Adam.

Let me explain what counterpart is. Your wife, like Eve was to Adam, is your peer. She is equal to you. She was not created from your head to your feet. She is not to be above you or below you. She is by your side like the rib she represents. She complements you. In other words, she is the finishing touch to your life. Your wife is to enrich your life and vice versa.

Just a few days ago, my mother told my son Justin very sternly and powerfully, "Justin, throw your eye at the right place and keep it there, being careful who you bring by your side as your wife." It took me by surprise what Justin's response was. He said, "Nonna, you know it. I want a godly woman and beautiful just like my mom."

What my mother was basically telling Justin was to set his eyes on the right woman and keep his eyes there until she becomes his wife. Ladies and Gentlemen, who you look at and who you entertain and whose attention you're trying to get will either bring you great joy or great sorrow.

What's so beautiful about the first couple, Adam and Eve, is that God was setting the standards for marriage, companionship, and partnership. After God created Eve, God brought Eve to Adam.

> Then the Lord God formed a woman from the rib that he
> had taken from the man. He brought her to the man.
>
> — GENESIS 2:22

It is God who brings our spouse to us. Not every person who comes to you should be your spouse. You must pray and wait for God to move. It is at this stage that many people make fatal mistakes. Like my mother said to my son, "Justin, throw your eye at the right place and keep it there, being careful who you bring by your side as your wife."

If you're a fisherman, you must keep rules and regulations to avoid losing your license. The fish you catch must be according to the rules. Many times, the fish just about makes those regulations. You might not see it with the physical eye. But when you weigh it, you will know. If the fish does not meet the regulations, you will have to throw the fish back into the sea. As fishy as it sounds, that analogy applies to us humans when we consider the most sacred act called marriage.

There is one primary thing every believer in Jesus Christ must remember: you absolutely cannot be unequally yoked with an unbeliever because the unbeliever can draw your heart away from God. Once this happens, there is no blessing because you stepped out of the will of God.

Forgiveness is a command. We are to forgive our spouse as Christ forgave us. The Bible is clear that God will not forgive us if we do not forgive others, including our spouse. Therefore, forgiveness is not an option but rather a must.

However, forgiveness doesn't mean you stay in an abusive relationship. Let me say very loud and clear, if your spouse cheats on you, you choose to forgive. And if your spouse continues to cheat, yes, you forgive. But Jesus gave adultery as a valid reason for divorce; therefore, adultery is biblical grounds for divorce. Please note, nowhere in the Bible does Jesus say forgive and stay when adultery is committed. All a spouse has to do is cheat once, and that is grounds for divorce.

In today's society, we have another major crisis. More and more people are coming out of the closet, identifying themselves as homosexuals. Automatically, that is grounds for divorce because it is an issue of abandonment, also biblical grounds for divorce. Sadly, some try to cover up their sin and deceive. There are some things a marriage cannot recover from; a spouse who has come out of the closet is one of those.

Some settle for a marriage where one spouse does not want to be intimate. This is dangerous because it puts the person wanting sex in a vulnerable position, ready to fall into temptation. This is abandonment and is biblical grounds for divorce.

Finally, nowhere in the Bible does it say you have to put up with spousal abuse. The first instinct God gave us is for survival. You do not have to stay in a marriage, nor should you want to, nor should you be forced to stay in a marriage, where your life is in jeopardy. In other words, if your spouse is physically abusing you, get out now!

You do not have to be beaten down physically, verbally, or emotionally. God can restore and rebuild anything that is broken. However, one major thing needs to occur before that happens; the people involved must surrender to God and invite God's will into their lives. God will not wrestle with man's will.

Christians act as if divorce is the ultimate sin in the Christian realm. No, it is not. There are situations and circumstances which leave people no choice but to end a marriage.

We found some common trends as we discussed each love story of real men and women in the Bible. We discovered it was the hand of God that led each couple to each other. We don't know the love story of Abraham and Sarah before their marriage. We do know they were from the same family, so they knew each other. However, we know how the other couples met.

What I enjoy about the love stories written in this book is how unique they are. Each one had challenges and disappointments. Yet, they could conquer the obstacles and trials that came their way. The testing each couple went through made them stronger and more powerful. Nothing that came against them could stand. The winds blew, and the storm raged. Uncertainties, disappointments, fears, cultural differences, age, health, plots, and schemes could not stand against them. Their love stories stood the test of time. There was no yelling, beating, cursing, or insults. There were no betrayals and no affairs. They faced their challenges and giants that came their way by putting their hope and trust in God. They came forth triumphant in the worst of situations, leaving a legacy of incredible and admirable love stories.

You and I can have the same love stories. They are achievable, and they do exist. I have found the secret to a happily ever after marriage. It is 100% bulletproof, successful, tried and true as we have seen it in the marriages of these six couples. It is easy and simple. Here it is:

> Love is patient. Love is kind. Love isn't jealous. It doesn't sing its own praises. It isn't arrogant. It isn't rude. It doesn't think about itself. It isn't irritable. It doesn't keep track of wrongs. It isn't happy when injustice is done, but it is happy with the truth. Love never stops being patient, never stops believing, never stops hoping, and never gives up. Love never comes to an end. There is the gift of speaking what God has revealed, but it will no longer be used. There is the gift of speaking in other languages, but it will stop by itself. There is the gift of knowledge, but it will no longer be used. Our knowledge is incomplete and our ability to speak what God has revealed is incomplete. But when what is complete comes, then what is incomplete will no longer be used. When I was a child, I spoke like a child, thought like a child, and reasoned like a child. When I became an adult, I no longer used childish ways. Now we see a blurred image in a mirror. Then we will see very clearly. Now my knowledge is incomplete. Then I will have complete knowledge as God has complete knowledge of me.
>
> — 1 CORINTHIANS 13:4-12

Within this passage, verse 11 stands out, *"When I was a child, I spoke like a child, thought like a child, and reasoned like a child. When I became an adult, I no longer used childish ways."* Let me explain, it wraps up everything just said about love. There comes a time when each person needs to grow up. You cannot remain like a child and act like a child in a relationship. Children don't reason. They want their own way, and they will stop at nothing to get it. They are selfish, self-centered, mean, and rude. They miss all the danger signs leading them to consequences, possibly harmful ones. Paul was saying what love is all about. It's about being patient and wanting what is best for the one you love. It's about honor, respect, and sacrificial giving. It is looking to the interest of your spouse above your own.

There is a difference between a child and a grown-up, a boy and a man, a girl and a woman. When you grow up you stop being like a child. That means you put away childish behaviors because now you are an adult and know right from wrong. Therefore, you act accordingly to the knowledge you have. This is what Paul meant as he clearly described what love is. There is nothing to add. It is self-explanatory.

There are lessons we can learn from these couples. Every single woman, except for Sarah (Remember Sarah and Abraham were already married when they were introduced in the Bible), was out and about. They were living their lives. None of them were looking for a husband. Guess where they were? They were out in the field working. Each woman's husband found them while they were working. They were confident, hard-working, strong, and self-sufficient.

Rebekah was busy getting water from the well. Rachel was busy getting water for her sheep. Ruth was out gathering grain. Esther was busy working on her beautification. The Shulamite was tending the vineyards. You don't see them wasting time and being idle. They had common sense, strength, dignity, a work ethic, and responsibility.

Additionally, they were God-fearing women who put God and His will before theirs. In other words, they were willing to do things God's way. Rebekah left her home to go to a far land to marry a man she had never met; she was more interested in doing the will of God. Rachel was willing to marry Jacob even after her father tricked him. Imagine her hurt knowing that the one she loved was tricked into marrying another woman, her sister. Imagine the tears that must have happened the day and night of the wedding when he married her sister. Ruth was willing to marry the older man from another culture. Ruth put aside all that she had known to marry Boaz. Esther married a divorced man and chose to follow the lead of the eunuch Hegai to fulfill the will of God, including the possibility of getting killed for standing up for her people. The Shulamite Woman was out in the vineyard working for her family. She left all that she knew behind to go live in the Palace with Solomon.

These were extremely beautiful women. They were women who honored God, their husbands, and their families. No wonder the hand of God led them and brought them before the eyes of these great men who became their husbands.

We often hear about the Proverbs 31 woman:

> Who can find a wife with a strong character? She is worth
>   far more than jewels. Her husband trusts her with all
>   his heart, and he does not lack anything good. She
>   helps him and never harms him all the days of her life.
> She seeks out wool and linen with care and works with
>   willing hands. She is like merchant ships. She brings
>   her food from far away. She wakes up while it is still
>   dark and gives food to her family and portions of food
>   to her female slaves.

She picks out a field and buys it. She plants a vineyard from the profits she has earned. She puts on strength like a belt and goes to work with energy. She sees that she is making a good profit. Her lamp burns late at night.

She puts her hands on the distaff, and her fingers hold a spindle. She opens her hands to oppressed people and stretches them out to needy people. She does not fear for her family when it snows because her whole family has a double layer of clothing. She makes quilts for herself. Her clothes are made of linen and purple cloth.

Her husband is known at the city gates when he sits with the leaders of the land.

She makes linen garments and sells them and delivers belts to the merchants. She dresses with strength and nobility, and she smiles at the future.

She speaks with wisdom, and on her tongue there is tender instruction. She keeps a close eye on the conduct of her family, and she does not eat the bread of idleness. Her children and her husband stand up and bless her.

Many women have done noble work, but you have surpassed them all!'

Charm is deceptive, and beauty evaporates, but a woman who has the fear of the Lord should be praised. Reward her for what she has done, and let her achievements praise her at the city gates.

— PROVERBS 31

Notice how she is an independent thinker, a proud woman. She continues to work and run her household, bringing up godly children and being a real helpmate to her husband. She brings him glory, honor, and respect before the city gates. That, ladies, is a real woman we all should aspire to be.

Each man, excluding Abraham (already married to Sarah), were men of integrity, character, honor, and self-respect. They weren't men who were out carousing, in and out of relationships. Isaac was 40 years old and out in the field working when the hand of God brought Rebekah to him. Jacob was coming in from a long journey and met Rachel at the well. Immediately, he fell in love. Boaz came into his fields riding on a horse to greet his men when he saw Ruth. Immediately, his eyes fell on her. Esther was brought into the King's chambers, and he immediately made her queen. He wasn't playing games. Solomon was overlooking his vineyards when his eyes caught sight of the Shulamite. The eyes of the men had been searching long for their wives. By His hand, God lovingly led the women before the eyes of these men. Each woman then became one with the man God led her to. This is the desire of God for every single woman or man.

Men, set your eyes on the right woman. This is why my mother said to my son, "Justin, throw your eye at the right place and keep it there." Because when you do that and when you're ready to mean business in marriage, there should be no room for you to fool around. To receive the blessing, you don't hurt other women in the process. You cast your eyes upon the one who will fulfill your every desire and meet your every expectation. You see, it was the hand of God that brought Eve to Adam, and it will be the hand of God that brings you your future spouse..

> Then the Lord God formed a woman from the rib that he
> had taken from the man. He brought her to the man,...

> — GENESIS 2:22

Ladies, it is your responsibility to live a life that honors you and your future spouse. It is said, "Behind every great man, there is a great woman." The success of your husband really does rely on you. Your actions and your attitude will either make or break your husband. Be concerned with living a life of integrity and good character. These women were out and about doing their daily work. They were living their lives. They were not out chasing men or paying attention to players. They waited for the right man to come along. Under no circumstance should you allow a guy to play with you and your emotions. Did you catch in these stories that immediately men claimed them as their wives? A man of character and goodwill toward you will not play with you. He will immediately claim you as his own. He will see your worth and what you bring to the table. He will not play games.

I would like to end this with my favorite Bible verse. When you play by the rules of God, God Himself, like He did for the Shulamite Woman, will bring you out into the arms of your husband.

> Who is this young woman coming from the wilderness
> with her arm around her beloved?

— SOLOMON 8:5

ACKNOWLEDGMENTS

This book would not have been possible without the wisdom, knowledge, and understanding of the Holy Spirit. I thank God that He entrusted me with a message to deliver that is in the center of the Lord's heart. Marriage is sacred. It is a promise that is made between a man and a woman. It is to be honored, treasured, and respected. There are preparations that need to be made before marriage, and we thank the Lord for revealing His truth that we penned.

We are grateful to Rise Up Publications Brian and Nina Paules who believe, encourage, and nourish us to write. This book was published because of them. Thank you. We thank Toby Marshall as proofreader and her validation of some of the culture and traditions of the Jewish faith. And most importantly, to Brian Hunter of Writing Solutions. We thank him for his expertise in the writing world. His dedication and support is greatly admired and respected by all of us. He is a highly anointed man with the gift of writing. I personally want to thank my children, Justin Noah Citro and Ellianna Destinee Citro, for supporting me by allowing the countless hours of seclusion to bring about this book.

Finally, we thank you, the readers, for purchasing this book with the intention of gaining the knowledge that lies in the Holy Scriptures to allow you to become the powerful spouse whom God created you to be.

ABOUT THE AUTHORS

Rev. Dr. Teresa Allissa Citro, PhD

Rev. Dr. Teresa Allissa Citro, PhD is the Chief Executive Officer of Learning Disabilities Worldwide. She is the President and Founder of Manda University. Dr. Citro is also the President and Founder of both Citro Cosmetics and Skincare as well as Citro Collections Fine Jewelry. Dr. Citro holds several graduate degrees, including a PhD in Education Leadership, a Doctorate in Religious Education, and a PhD in Corporate Leadership. She is a well-respected authority in the field of Education/Special Education. She has written extensively in the areas of education, counseling, parenting, and Christian theology. She is the Co-Editor of two respected peer-reviewed journals on Special Education. She is the Editor-In-Chief of Everyday Life Magazine. She is the creator and co-host of the program Light of the World. Dr. Citro has received many awards for her contributions in the field of Special Education and was awarded the prestigious Presidential Lifetime Achievement Award in 2021. Dr. Citro is also a worldwide public speaker.

Dr. Nicholas D. Young, PhD

Dr. Nicholas D. Young, PhD has worked in diverse roles for over 30 years, serving as a teacher, principal, counselor, special education director, graduate professor, graduate program director, graduate dean, and longtime superintendent of schools. He holds several graduate degrees, including a PhD in educational administration and an EdD in psychology. He served in the US Army and Army Reserves for over 36 years, commanding several large military units before retiring at the rank of Colonel. He was named the Massachusetts Superintendent of the Year. He earned several civilian and military awards, including the General Douglas MacArthur Leadership Award, the Vice-Admiral Haywood Scholarship Award, the Presidential Lifetime Achievement Award, the SAR Veteran Service Award, and the highly coveted Legion of Merit for exemplary service to the nation. Dr. Young has authored dozens of books, book chapters, and articles in the fields of education, counseling, and psychology.

Linda A. Knowles, PhD

Linda A. Knowles, PhD, M.Div. is the Executive Director of Thread of Hope, Inc. Dr. Knowles is also the Vice President of Academic Affairs and Dean of Theology at Manda University. She is a Professor of Theology. She has authored books and written periodicals and blogs extensively on Christian theology, counseling, and godly living. Dr. Knowles has traveled on several mission trips throughout the world.

www.threadofhope.org

 twitter.com/Threadofhope7

CPSIA information can be obtained
at www.ICGtesting.com
Printed in the USA
BVHW051722260422
635365BV00007B/671